How to Survive Your Mother

BY THE SAME AUTHOR

How to Make Your Million from the Internet
(and what to do if you don't)

Eva Cassidy: Her True Story
(with Rob Burley)

Flop Idol

Vote for . . . Who?

TV broadcaster Jonathan Maitland reported for Radio 4's *Today* programme for six years before moving to BBC 1's *Watchdog*. He currently works for ITV as a reporter on the *Tonight* programme with Trevor McDonald, and has presented other popular ITV shows, including *House of Horrors* and *Vote for Me*.

How to Survive Your Mother

A TRUE STORY

JONATHAN MAITLAND

**SIMON &
SCHUSTER**

London · New York · Sydney · Toronto

A CBS COMPANY

First published in Great Britain by Simon & Schuster UK Ltd, 2006
A CBS COMPANY

Copyright © Jonathan Maitland, 2006

3 5 7 9 10 8 6 4 2

Simon & Schuster UK Ltd
Africa House
64–78 Kingsway
London WC2B 6AH

www.simonsays.co.uk

Simon & Schuster Australia
Sydney

A CIP catalogue record for this book
is available from the British Library

ISBN 0-7432-1998-8

Typeset in Sabon by M Rules
Printed and bound in Great Britain
by William Clowes Ltd, Beccles, Suffolk

Foreword

Whenever I get a Big Idea, for a book or a TV programme, there always seems to be a piece of cake in the vicinity. In this case, inspiration struck in the presence of a large slice of lemon drizzle in the summer of 1992. I was with someone called Rachel Johnson and we were bunking off school at a café round the corner from Broadcasting House in Oxford Circus. We were both BBC radio reporters: she worked for *The World Tonight* and I was on the *Today* programme, which was based in the neighbouring office. We got to talking about our families. She told me about her brother – a blond-haired, eccentric, would-be Tory MP called Boris – and I repaid her with tales about my mother. After I'd rattled off a few stock stories, Rachel looked impressed. And amused. And shocked.

'If you can write it as well as you tell it,' she said, 'it would make a great book.'

I've been meaning to write it ever since. But it has turned out very differently from how I envisaged it. At first it was going to be a (hopefully) entertaining collection of amusing and outrageous anecdotes. But a chance meeting with a journalist changed all that and set the book off on quite a different course. As you are about to find out.

It was well before the lemon drizzle cake episode, however, that I first began to realize that I had what appeared to be an unusually interesting mother. It was the start of the eighties and I was studying law at King's College London. Word had got around that she was a source of rich entertainment. I would spend hours in the students' union bar, surrounded by an enthralled circle of friends, telling story after story about her. As the evenings progressed jaws would move steadily southwards. Some of them accused me of making it up. I wasn't. I can understand why they thought that, though. A story about an apparently sane, successful businesswoman who suddenly decides to navigate her way through an inner-city traffic jam by driving her bright green Mini along the pavement and then emerges in just a dressing gown, cackling triumphantly, ready to do the supermarket shopping, smacks of embellishment. Likewise the tale about her sudden announcement to the newspapers that she had six months to live and was opening a hotel for homosexuals in the middle of the north Surrey commuter belt. But then they started to meet her. Or rather experience her and be exposed to her. And then they started to realize that, yes, this was the kind of woman who could easily have started a conversation with my brother's girlfriend – whom she was meeting for the first time – with a quizzical look, a pause and the question: 'Why don't you have plastic surgery on your nose?'

I never thought she was particularly unusual, mind you. But then, for obvious reasons, I had no yardsticks with which to measure her eccentricities. So I used to take it entirely in my stride when, asked what she thought of my 16-year-old best friend, she replied, without drawing breath: 'He is a superficial c***.'

It was only, as I say, at university, when a friend stopped me in the canteen and begged me to 'tell us a story about your mum, Jonny, go on, just a quick one', that I started to realize that my mother was perhaps a bit different.

I hesitated for months before starting this book. I was worried that it was too self-indulgent. Who wants to read a book by a forty-something TV reporter about his relationship with his mother? But then came the conversation that gave me good reason to go at it from an additional and very different angle. It turned into something more than just a memoir, a life story. And without wanting to sound pretentious, anyone who loves writing craves good stories. So it seemed a bit perverse to sit atop a mountain of vivid, remarkable tales and not write them down. I also – and I hope this doesn't sound presumptuous – thought it might bring welcome feelings of empathy and even comfort to those who, like me, have had – and still do – complex, difficult and traumatic relationships with their mothers (i.e. just about everyone). But it was only when Simon and Schuster, the publishers of this book, convinced me that there would be interest in my story that I decided to bung it all down. This isn't just a book about my mother, though: it's about what it feels like to find out things about her that I wasn't really supposed to know.

Finally, a word about veracity. This isn't just 'based on a true story', as they like to say in Hollywood, often misleadingly. Everything in the following pages happened. In the interests of other people's privacy, however, and to protect the guilty as well as the innocent, some names, dates and locations have been changed.

Jonathan Maitland
February 2006

One day in July 1973

My mother was dead. She had just died. Right there and then, in her bed, in front of me. There appeared to be no doubt about it. A few seconds earlier she had been gripping my hand in hers and moaning instructions in between audible gasps of what I took to be pain. She then whispered what seemed very much like her last words: 'The money . . . uuuuurrrgh . . . is in the bottom drawer.' Her hand went limp and her head slumped back slightly into the pillow. Rather too deliberately, now I come to think about it.

She lay there motionless. I was too young at the time – just gone twelve – to notice that there was something rather too theatrical about it all. The way her hand suddenly and dramatically loosened its grasp on mine. The way it began its slow and purposeful slide down the side of the bed, where it was eventually left dangling. The way her eyelids flickered shut. Her final sigh.

In years to come I would become familiar with these Performances Intended to Signify Imminent Death. But at the time my only reference points in these matters were dramatic deathbed scenes from movies. And on that basis, my mother had most definitely passed away, albeit minus a tastefully

orchestrated soundtrack. And so my immature little world came
to an end, at about half past seven on a weekday summer's
evening, the tears flowing quickly and thickly.

Lord knows how long I stayed there, perched on the side of her
large double bed, staring at her dead face. Curiously rational
thoughts started to appear in my head, like car headlights through
the rain. Such as: 'What should I do now?' and 'Money? What
money? How much? And which bottom drawer, exactly?' Finally,
I realized I had better tell someone. I went downstairs, trying to
work out who I should report my mother's death to. It was a difficult one. There were plenty of candidates to choose from. My
home was a hotel and there were plenty of guests in the bar and
the dining room. I considered, for a moment, sharing the news
with one of them. It didn't seem an odd thing to do as I had spent
most of my childhood, when I wasn't at boarding school, living in
a variety of guest houses or old people's homes owned by my parents. I had become used to the kindness of strangers. In the end I
told the hotel manageress, whom I found hovering at the back of
the kitchen. She said nothing and rushed past me, through the
dining room, up the stairs and into the bedroom.

She took one look at the corpse, which, I noticed, was in a
slightly different position from the one it had been in earlier, and
dialled 999. 'Hello? Ambulance? Come now please. Nonsuch
Park Hotel, 357 London Road, Ewell . . . somebody has . . . it's
an emergency . . . I don't know, I'm looking at her now and it's
not good so just come, will you? . . . thank you.'

Three of them, all uniformed, walked into my mother's bedroom. One took her hand just below the wrist.

'She's got a pulse.'

I didn't know what that meant. Was she dead? Or alive? Or
what?

'We're going to have to take her in. Get the gear.' The ambulance man gestured to his two colleagues, who left the room immediately. Then I saw something. At least I thought I did. It looked as if one of my mother's eyelids had flickered. Then again, maybe not. Hold on a minute, there it goes again. It can't be . . . she's dead! Maybe it was this rigor mortis thing I'd heard about at school. Hold on, though. . .isn't that when the body goes stiff? That's not what's happening here. Hold on again. Her jaw is moving. She is making a noise, I think. A small groan-cum-murmur. Now she is trying to say something.

'Not . . . want . . . to . . . go . . . to hospital . . .'

She's alive! She is definitely alive! But how can that be?

She was dead. She *was* dead, in fact. She had died, right here in front of me. But now here she is, stirring, murmuring, breathing. What is going on? Strangely, I felt slightly disappointed. It was as if I had been cheated. The ambulance man who had been taking her pulse still had her hand in his. He spoke to her softly. 'No, come on, Mrs Maitland. You are clearly very ill. You must come with us.'

'No . . . not want to go . . .'

Clearly, this was a tricky one. She didn't, for reasons best known to her, want to go to hospital. Possibly because there was nothing wrong with her. But then again she couldn't start making a lively, cogent, impassioned speech about why she didn't want to go when a few minutes earlier she had done a mightily convincing impression of someone irrevocably headed for the St Helier hospital mortuary. I was bewildered. I left the room and headed for one of my favourite destinations – the hotel's dessert trolley. More specifically, its trifle bowl.

I was well into my second helping when the manageress appeared at my shoulder.

'I think she's better now, your mother. Thank the Lord.'

'I thought she was dead. She died, didn't she?'

'I don't know. But she wants cheesecake now, for everyone.'

She took a virgin strawberry cheesecake as big as one of the cymbals on a drum kit from the bottom shelf of the trolley, cut four huge slices, put them on a tray and headed upstairs.

I began to hear the sound of voices being raised. Not in anger or sorrow, but joy. One of them was my mother's. I slid back upstairs. I entered the room unnoticed. My mother was sitting up in bed, holding a plate of half-eaten cheesecake, telling a story to the ambulance men. It was going down well. Everyone was laughing now. She was glowing. In her slightly accented English – she sounded a little Spanish – she was telling a story I had heard several times before. The one about the man from the local council who had written to tell her that Nonsuch Park Hotel guests were not allowed to leave their cars in the park opposite, overnight. She was well into her stride now.

'So I write back to him. And do you know what I say in letter? I say: "Dear sir. Why do you think people go to the park? So their dogs can shit everywhere. Yes. All their dogs do is shit and piss. But my guests don't. They are very clean. They just park their cars there. So why don't you complain about the people who shit and piss everywhere, instead of my guests, who never leave a mess? It's very simple. You know what you can do. Yours sincerely, Mrs Maitland." And you know what? I never hear from him again!'

I couldn't work out what was so funny about all this but the cheesecake-munching ambulance men loved it.

'Remarkable woman, your mother,' said one of them, as they brushed past me on their way out of the room.

'Very brave. Very brave indeed. Extraordinary.'

9 September 2004

'Here he comes! Quick!'

I had spent the last seventy-five minutes staring at him across a crowded courtroom and now here he was, walking out of Lewes magistrates' court towards me. This was to be our programme's Big Moment – the bit where I confront him. The villain. I always like to get things in perspective when I doorstep conmen: although they may have caused suffering and distress, they're not exactly up there with war criminals, axe murderers and child killers in the Evil Hall of Fame. Tone, therefore, is all-important. There's no point in treating someone as if they've gassed six million Kurdish refugees when all they've done is overcharge someone for fixing their faulty boiler. So as he walked towards me and I got my opening line ready, I mentally briefed myself to be firm but not hysterically outraged. The audience isn't stupid, I told myself, as he came closer. They know he's a scumbag, you don't have to go over the top on him. Nevertheless, as baddies go, he was still a pretty filthy piece of work. His name was Gary Seabrook and he was a dodgy plumber. He had conned a desperately ill old lady, living on her own, out of her life savings. There are always

details that stick in your mind in cases like these. In this particular one it was the way that Seabrook – a cold-eyed,
shaven-headed man in his late twenties – had gone about his
business. He actually drove his victim down to her local high
street and then virtually frog-marched her to the cashpoint,
where he made her take out £400. By the time he'd finished, he'd
taken £5,300 from her: all the money she had in the world.
Twenty minutes earlier he had been found guilty on six counts of
deception but had been let out on bail to await sentencing. And
here he was, right now, in front of me and a small pack of journalists, all armed with notepads and microphones.

'Mr Seabrook . . . Jonathan Maitland from *Tonight with
Trevor McDonald*. I just want to ask you about the way you've
behaved. Why choose a woman in her seventies, living on her
own, to rip off? Why not pick on someone your own size?'

He completely ignored me and carried on walking.
Fortunately we were on a long stretch of pavement and there
were no buildings for him to escape into. I could tell he was
dying to punch me: his heavily tattooed knuckles were clenched
and his shoulders, encased in a cheap and shiny blue suit for the
occasion, were twitching. Normally, I am the world's biggest
coward. If you put me in a situation like this without a camera
crew in attendance, I would run a mile the moment someone like
Seabrook bared their teeth. But there's something about the presence of a camera lens which fills me with a fleeting sense of
bravery. Or bravado. I had another go.

'Mr Seabrook . . . aren't you even going to apologize for what
you've done? To Wendy's relatives, even?'

His victim – Eileen Simpson – had died soon after the full
extent of Seabrook's rip-off had become clear to her. Again,
Seabrook said nothing. His lawyer spoke instead. Excellent! A
chance for some interaction.

'He is entitled not to say anything.'

'I know. And the relatives are equally entitled to an explanation, aren't they? I mean, come on, Mr Seabrook: don't you realize that by not saying anything to us, people are just going to think you're even more of a lying, thieving scumbag than you already are?'

Shit. I had broken my golden rule. I had no need to gratuitously insult him like that. I should have remained neutral. Now, arguably, I had vacated a little bit of the moral high ground by letting my emotions get the better of me. There was more than just a hint of accusation in my voice, and some viewers might think I'd gone over the top because I had sounded just too outraged. But then again, I was outraged. Unusually so. Funny that. Normally, in cases like these, I remain reasonably cool and professionally detached. Having said that, it worked: Seabrook could contain himself no longer. He lurched towards me and I instinctively flinched backwards, anticipating an imminent meeting with his right fist.

'I tell you one fing . . . I am not a scumbag, all right?'

This was good.

'OK then, how would you describe yourself? How would you describe someone who rips off an old lady to the tune of five thousand pounds, when all she's got is a blocked drain? A blocked drain that costs maybe a hundred quid to fix, at most?'

'I . . . am . . . not . . . a . . . scumbag. All right?'

We had reached the end of the road, literally. I couldn't carry on the conversation trying to cross a very busy Lewes High Street as we might have ended up under a truck. And we had enough footage for the programme anyway, so I let him go. The camera crew, my producer and I walked slowly back to the courthouse, conducting a post mortem as we went. They were happy but I was mildly disappointed, on the grounds of inappropriate tone. They told me I was being paranoid and not to worry. As we talked, I noticed a figure just ahead of us whom I vaguely recognized. He glanced back at me at least twice in the space of twenty seconds.

This is my job, then: I am a so-called 'investigative TV reporter'. I spend most of my time reporting and presenting programmes about rogues, conmen and charlatans. Dodgy tradesmen who nick your money and piss in your sink when they think you're not looking. Company executives who cook the books and raid their employees' pension fund. Along the way I've done programmes on cigarette smugglers, car thieves and mortgage swindlers. As you may have gathered, I tend to specialize in the slightly sleazy end of the market. I don't know why. I've always loved a good con. Or rather, telling the story of one. Sometimes I even find myself quite admiring the inventiveness of the people who pull off the scams. Many is the time I've felt, about a particularly imaginative and ingenious mortgage swindler, for instance, 'There goes a potential chancellor of the exchequer.' I've always been fascinated by that nature/nurture argument. What makes someone do bad things? Are some people born that way? Or is it learned behaviour? Or is there a Moment When, as in a Moment When the previously honest rogue/criminal/charlatan decides to take the fork in the road signposted 'Dodgy' as opposed to 'Honest'?

Our programme about Mr Seabrook, however, wasn't going to concern itself with such niceties. It was simply going to be a straight retelling of his various crimes and misdemeanours. Which is why we needed some more shots of Lewes magistrates' court. Which is why we were now standing outside said building, with not much to do, while the cameraman did his stuff. Just then I felt a tap on the arm. It was the bloke who'd been just ahead of us on the pavement, the one who had glanced back at me a couple of times. Close up, I realized I knew him. He was a hack. I'd seen him around a few times at journalistic 'events' like this and we would sometimes exchange the smallest of talk, but I didn't know his name and I was pretty sure he didn't know mine. This was because we came from different sides of the Great Journalistic Divide. I was in TV, he was a print journalist. There is a low-level, mutual professional hostility between the two camps, which is clearly not the most fertile of flower beds for friendships to blossom in. Which is why, although I'd known him for years, I didn't actually *know* him. Or like him. But now, for the first time, he seemed to be taking an interest in me. In fact he was looking at me in a way in which he had never looked at me before. I tried to remember his name. I thought it may have been Peter but I didn't want to risk it so I gave him the safety greeting – a smile, a nod and an 'all right, mate?'

'Yes, all right, thanks.'

He looked like a classic Fleet Street hack of the old school – regulation grey mac (lightly stained), fraying suit bought from Dunn and Co. between 1971 and 1979, and of course the ever-present wire-bound notepad with chewed Biro slotted through the binding at the top. The type who would still have doggedly used a typewriter even though they'd been obsolete for years. His face was rough, red and veiny, like rare roast beef.

'Well done there, mate,' he said. 'I was taking notes when you doorstepped him. One or two useful quotes there, I think.'

'Thanks. Yes, I can see the headline. SCUMBAG: WHY I AM NOT A SCUMBAG perhaps. Do I get royalties?'

'Ha ha ha. No. Here ... did you say your name was Maitland, back there?'

'Yes, that's right. Jonathan. Jonathan Maitland. Why?'

I felt uncomfortable. I'm used to homing in on other people – I do it for a living – but I'm not that keen when it's the other way round.

'D'your family come from Epsom, you know, Surrey, round there?' he said. He wasn't looking me in the eye, I noticed.

'Yes, they do . . . how d'you know?'

'I worked there once. Local papers. Sixties and seventies. The *Advertiser*, *Surrey Herald*, things like that.'

'Oh . . . right.'

He lowered a bucket into the mental well of his memory.

'Maitland . . . Maitland . . .'

'Correct. Maitland. Thank you for reminding me.'

'No, it's just that . . . er, is that the same Maitland who . . . were you . . . I mean, are you, related to . . . people who . . . were in business, there, back then?'

'Yes, my parents ran hotels and old people's homes and stuff like that, if that's what you're talking about.'

'Right . . . right.'

The hack with the roast beef face seemed to be doing a lot of thinking.

'Here . . . d'you know, I think I remember it now. Maitland! Your parents got into a bit of trouble in the sixties, didn't they? With the hotels and the old people's homes, stuff like that.'

'Er . . . I'm not sure. Not that I know.'

'Oh.' He seemed disappointed. 'I'm pretty sure something dodgy went on . . . Still. Never mind. See you. Cheers.'

'Cheers.'

If that exchange had occurred between two normal people – i.e. not reporters – there would have been embarrassment and awkwardness. In fact had we been normal, he wouldn't even have said what he said in the first place. But when you're reporters it's hard not to treat people and their feelings as commodities. Because they're not people and feelings at all. Not real ones. They're just Stories, aren't they? Stuff to write about or make a programme on. Plane crash? Great story! Local company goes bust, leaving hundreds out of work? Great story! So rather than feeling embarrassed or awkward, I was intrigued. Clearly, my parents were once a great story. But why?

One summer evening, 1967

'm not keen on books that tell stories of unhappy child-
hoods. You know the ones: brought up in a kennel, whipped
ten times day and forced to eat stale dog food while the
mother and father lark about in their best devil-worshipping
gear. Each successive tale of woe seems like an attempt to
outdo the previous one. Like that Monty Python sketch where
a group of successful Yorkshiremen sit round a table saying
stuff like: 'You think you 'ad it 'ard? Well, let me tell you
summat. When we were kids, our dad would kill us, every
night, before we went to bed, and chop us into a thousand tiny
pieces.'

OK, that's the disclaimer. So please don't accuse me of being
a hypocrite when I tell you about my earliest memory. I'm not
dredging it up to make you feel sorry for me, or for dramatic
effect, I'm just telling it how it happened. Last week, before that
Curious Incident of the Hack in the Daytime, the soup of my
memory had been lying undisturbed for some time. But then
Roast Beef Hack came along, plunged a ladle in and gave it a
good stir. As a result some interesting bits have floated to the
surface. The oldest ingredient – the earliest and most vivid

memory of all – comes from a jar marked '1967'. That was when my mother tried to kill herself outside the London Hilton. Actually, it's an image more than a memory, really: her head, slumped over the steering wheel of her Rover, with blood pouring from it. I have a reasonably clear recollection of how she'd got there. Minutes earlier she'd had a massive argument with my father, over chicken sandwiches, in the coffee shop at the Hilton. I don't mean the argument was about chicken sandwiches, by the way – that's what we were eating at the time. In fact I'm not sure what it was about. I may not remember how it started, but I know how it ended.

'OK, Irving,' she said, her jaw setting into something like tungsten. 'If you don't agree . . . I kill myself. Now.'

'Go on, then.'

Cut to ten minutes later. There I am, standing on the thin stretch of pavement in the middle of the busy road outside the London Hilton. Cars are whizzing this way and that. I am seven years old. I am with a small group of people who are about to cross the road. I don't know how I got there, but I know that I don't know any of them. We all become aware of a stationary car revving up in the distance about a hundred yards away. The sound gets louder and louder and suddenly the car jerks forward and sets off with a screech. Someone says something. Something like: 'She's going a bit fast, isn't she?' None of us moves. The car is indeed going very fast. It is heading straight for the railings that surround the roundabout's grassy central reservation to our right. I realize that, yes, the car is going to smash into the roundabout, at speed, with my mother in it. Just like they do on the telly. Just like on Z Cars.

The railings did better than the car: they stayed more or less intact. The front bonnet of the Rover did not. My mother was unconscious. Blood was running down her forehead, which was on the steering wheel, motionless. I turned to the man next to me, whom I'd never seen before and haven't seen since.

'She's dead,' I said. 'She's my mum.'

7 October 2004

Another day, another doorstep, another courthouse. This time it was King's Lynn and my quarry was a very large and very rich young man called Michael Carroll, who was facing a charge of possessing Class A drugs. On occasions such as these, when there is a lot of sitting around and waiting involved, my preferred time-filling options – in no particular order – are:

1) Read the *Daily Mail*
2) Play Scrabble on my laptop
3) Eat sandwiches and/or cakes
4) Text at random.

On this morning I had gone for a combo of 1) and 3). Now sometimes, on jobs like this, you worry that the person you're waiting for will pass by unnoticed. Or that your cameraman will shove his lens in the face of someone unconnected with the events in question. I once accused someone, on camera, of being a callous fraudster who had cheated more than a dozen pensioners out of their life savings. He turned out to be the assistant manager of the local supermarket on a day off. His only crime was to have looked – a bit, from 30 yards away – like the bloke I was supposed to be doorstepping. There was going to be no such problem today. There weren't many people in the world who looked like Michael Carroll. His distinguishing features included the word 'EVIL', tattooed in large black letters on to the back of his fat, red neck. He also weighed around 18 stone – or close on 19, if you included the bulky bits of jewellery strapped round, pierced through and dangling from various bits of his body. Carroll was not what you would call a law-abiding citizen: he had almost as many criminal convictions to his name as he did bits of bling. But it wasn't just those convictions, or today's drugs allegations, which had brought us – i.e. the media – there that day. Our interest in Mr Carroll was down to the fact that he was, courtesy of the tabloids, 'The Lotto Lout'. Six months earlier he'd been a car mechanic earning 200 quid a week. Then, in the time it takes to make a cup of tea, he found himself £13,000,000 richer. He was now earning, I'd calculated, two thousand pounds a day in interest payments alone. I had been trying, for the last month, to get him to do an interview, on camera, for the *Tonight* programme. He'd let me down four times so far, always at the last moment. But now I was in a position to at least get some usable footage of him.

'Is that him?' someone shouted, as a large, baseball-capped man emerged from the courthouse.

'Nah,' shouted someone else. 'Not enough bling.'

I recognized that last voice. I turned to see whose it was and identified its owner immediately. Roast Beef was on the menu again. We clocked each other. Just then another shout went up.

'Here he comes!'

The phalanx of about twenty-five reporters, cameramen and

paparazzi surged forward like a swarm of bees. Once Carroll saw us he gave his customary greeting, a grunted 'Fuck off, the lot of yer!', coupled with his familiar two-fingered salute. Within seconds he had got into the back of a car and been driven off at high speed. Not the in-depth interview I was after, but we had at least filmed it all. As the cameraman, sound lady, producer and I made our way back to our van, I saw Roast Beef Face again a few yards ahead. He was sitting on a wall talking into his mobile. We acknowledged each other. I told the crew to go on and sat on the wall near, but not next to, him. He glanced over and mouthed the words 'Sorry, busy, can't talk'. I nodded. You're not getting rid of me that easily, I thought. I got up off the wall but hovered, making sure not to catch his eye. Once he'd finished, I made my move.

'All right, mate?' I said.

'Yeah, fine. You?'

'Not bad. He's good value, isn't he?'

'Brilliant. Made for us.'

'Here, you know that stuff you were talking about the other day, about my parents and all that . . . what was that about?'

'Oh . . . yes. I can't remember exactly but it was all pretty grubby.'

'Ah. Yeah, I know what you're talking about. My mum used to build stuff without planning permission and the council got well fucked off. Quite funny.'

'Er . . . It was a lot worse than that, I think.'

'Like . . . what?'

'Your parents – they ran old people's homes, didn't they?'

'Yes, before they both got into hotels.'

'But they stopped running old people's homes, didn't they?'

'Obviously.'

'But . . . do you know *why* they stopped running them?'

He began to look awkward. We appeared to be entering choppy waters.

'No, not really. More money in hotels, I guess.'

He said nothing.

'Look . . . things . . . happened. That were . . . interesting. It was quite big news, locally.'

'Really? Like what?'

'Don't you know?'

'No. Not unless you tell me.'

'Look, it's not really my job to tell you. It wasn't . . . really very good, let's put it that way. You're a journalist, do some digging. It shouldn't be that difficult. Or just ask your parents. If you haven't already.'

1968–71

After the London Hilton Chicken Sandwich Suicide Attempt, my mother was rushed to hospital. She survived but the marriage didn't. Soon after she returned home with her head swathed in bandages, my father disappeared from my life. That wasn't difficult, mind you, as I hardly ever saw him anyway. I have virtually no childhood memories of him whatsoever. For a start, I was away at boarding school a lot of the time: I was sent to one in Dorking, called High Trees, when I was three. And even when I was at home, he and my mother always seemed to be 'busy with the business'. Not long after my mother 'got rid of Irving' (her phrase, not mine) his place was taken by someone else: my soon-to-be stepfather, Dennis.

Dennis. Dennis was a good bloke. Everyone thought Dennis was a good bloke. He was, to trot out a cliché, like a father to me. I might remember little or nothing about my real father but there are plenty of images of Dennis. Tall, solidly built, dark-haired and good-looking in a rakish, Jack the Lad kind of way. Had a fair pair of sideburns on him. Good sense of humour, very sociable. Bit of a cockney accent. Loved laughing, drinking, John Wayne, Dean Martin and James Bond. Modelled himself on them a bit, I think. Came from Lewisham in south-east London, supported Charlton Athletic. Soon after he came into my life, he told me it was time for me to have a football team too. We wrote down all the names of the London sides on different bits of paper, scrunched them up and put them in a tea mug. I picked Charlton Athletic. He took me to my first game: the Valley, naturally. Not a bad player himself. He used to be in the same side as my brother Pete. A big, no-nonsense centre half, in the Jack Charlton mould: not much skill, but good in the air, got the job done. It was he, and only he, who used to write to me regularly at boarding school, in that clear, friendly, honest italic writing of his. The letters used to begin 'Dear Ketchup . . .' on account of my predilection for having it with everything, even curry. He once sent me thirty-six Mars Bars in a parcel. We weren't allowed sweets at school. I remember the headmaster, a man with hairy nostrils and scarily dark eyebrows, shaking the parcel before giving it to me, saying, 'I hope it's not tuck, Maitland.'

Dennis was a member of the Household Cavalry. I remember that because he used to show me pictures of him dressed up in all the gear. Very impressive. Red tunic, fancy helmet with plenty of plumage and white trousers tucked into big black boots that went right up to his knees. He used to take part in the Changing of the Guard, he did. Then he became a policeman. He used to enthral me with his stories. Like the time he had to deal with the aftermath of a particularly bad road accident and all that was left of the driver was a thumb on the steering wheel.

By the time he met my mother Dennis was working as a private detective. He met her on a job, I seem to remember. He had a gun, I think. Not that he was a good shot. He once came home from work, suitably refreshed after a visit to the pub, to find me bending over at the bottom of our garden. I had a target, like the one they have in archery competitions, pinned to my unusually large 7-year-old arse. My brother Pete had just been given an airgun for his birthday and was using me as target practice. I didn't really mind: I was glad of the attention. I was less happy a few minutes later when Pete persuaded Dennis to have a pop himself. He shot me in the thigh, wounding me severely. I was rushed to hospital and he had to explain it to my mother. 'Sorry, I've just shot your youngest son in the leg, but I was actually aiming at his arse' would have covered it, but it must have been tricky.

Dennis used to spend a lot of time 'down the Queen Vic' in North Cheam, a south London suburb which was, and still is, stunningly anonymous. An architectural and cultural desert. There's only one good view of North Cheam, local wags used to say. The one you get in your rear-view mirror.

'Where is Dennis?' my mother would shout.

'Down the Queen Vic,' would come the reply from various members of staff, like a congregation replying to a vicar. For a while I actually thought the pub was called the Down the Queen Vic.

Hmm. The Queen Vic. That's where he'd been just before he shot me in the leg. Appropriate, really. Just like another over-the-top soap, much of the central action in my mother's relationship with Dennis took place in, near or because of the Queen Vic. He was no Dirty Den, though: he was far too good-natured for that. Just as in the TV show, however, the pair of them were only ever seconds from the next volcanic argument or dramatic show-down. I can't remember what caused the bust-ups but the recipe was usually the same: take one or two tablespoons of blood and add several large portions of shouting and screaming. Leave mixture to settle, then top it off with a lovey-dovey reunion. Repeat the whole thing again the next day.

Then, all of a sudden, Dennis disappeared from my life, just like my dad. The last time I saw him was more than twenty years ago when I was a BBC trainee radio reporter and I interviewed him for a documentary about private detectives. He's now living in Spain with his wife and two grown-up kids. His son is called Dean after Dean Martin. I've been meaning to see him for years. We started writing to each other a while back and he's invited me out there several times. I've got even more reason to go now. He, surely, must know what the hack with the roast beef face is talking about. Or rather isn't. There are gaps to be filled and dots to be joined up. Spain, here I come.

18–20 February 2005 and
1968–71 revisited

Dennis picked me up at Malaga airport. When I knew him he looked a bit like Lee Brilleaux, the imposing lead singer of Dr Feelgood, the seminal seventies R 'n' B band from Southend. Now, thirty odd years on, the first thing I noticed about the 72-year-old Dennis was his hair. It was thinner, lanker and clumpier than it used to be. But there was a reason for that and it had nothing to do with old age. He had just survived a horrendous bout of stomach and bowel cancer. He had to grind his way through several months of chemotherapy, he told me in the car on the way to his villa, as well as an operation that left a corking, Frankenstein's Monster-style scar down the middle of his belly, more than a foot long. The chemotherapy had played havoc with his gums, hence the loss of a good many teeth. He'd forgotten to put his top set of dentures in, so he had a large gap where his two front ones used to be. Despite the orthodontic and tonsorial peculiarities, however, he looked – the tan helped – surprisingly healthy.

He and his family had moved to Malaga – or, to be precise,

Torre del Mar, about an hour's drive from the city's airport – for
the usual reasons. Sun and money. Compared to where he and
his wife Sue had been living (just outside Norwich) their newly
acquired villa in southern Spain got a lot more of the former and
cost a lot less of the latter. He loved it here, he said. He wasn't
ever going back. The villa took some getting to. Once you'd left
the main road you had to drive for ten minutes, uphill, over a
rough and rocky dirt track. Talk about wide open spaces. The
higher we climbed, the more of the burnt Spanish landscape I
could see. It was as brown and dry as crispbread. Occasionally,
every half a mile or so, we'd come across a villa. 'The bloke who
used to be in Foreigner, the American rock group, lives there,'
said Dennis, a bend or two before turning into his own driveway. Within minutes of getting out of the car we were sitting on
his porch – he with a large gin and tonic, I noticed, nostalgic-
ally – gazing at the reason that would keep him here for the rest
of his life. I've never seen a mountain range look, or be, so naturally lit as the one that dominates the entire view from Dennis's
garden. It was purple here, blue there, majestic and dominant.

'Beats North Cheam, dunnit?' he said, with that familiar Sid
James laugh of his. He was frailer now. He used to be so imposing. John Wayne, the big tough cowboy, had given a fair bit of
ground to Blakey, the conductor from *On the Buses*.

'Right,' I said. 'Let's start at the beginning. There's a lot I want
to ask you. So don't hold back.'

No one can accuse my mother or Dennis of starting their relationship while she was still married. Oh no. They met, for the
very first time, after her marriage was over. Roughly thirty seconds after it was over. Dennis, it turns out, was the private
investigator who'd been employed by my mother's lawyer, a
flamboyant and very tall (6 foot 8 inches) bloke called

Humphrey Benson, to 'handle' the nuts and bolts of the case. This, in effect, meant doing the dirty work. In those days, you see, you couldn't get divorced as easily as you can now. You had to 'prove' that one or other of the parties had committed adultery. My mother, who according to Dennis was much more keen on the idea of a divorce than my father, decided that it was to be my father who had committed the non-existent adultery. As a result, Dennis was engaged by the flamboyant and very tall Mr Humphrey Benson to get a signed confession from my father saying he had been having an affair with our Spanish maid, Maria. Even though he hadn't. Dennis then had to stand up in court on the day the case was heard and confirm that Mr Irving Bernard Maitland had confessed to an affair. Once the relevant bits of paperwork had been signed, sealed and delivered by the judge sitting in the family division of the High Court in the Strand on 23 April 1968, the marriage was over. There was, however, an unusual amount of press interest in the case of Maitland versus Maitland: this was the first time in British legal history that a divorce had been granted without the need for both sides to employ very expensive barristers to plead their case in the courtroom. As a result there were a fair few hacks hanging around outside wanting a quote from my parents. The very tall and flamboyant Humphrey Benson didn't want my mother to be hassled so he asked Dennis to look after her and get her home safely. So, within a minute of the case being over, Dennis introduced himself to the newly single Mrs Maitland and suggested they slip out of the back of the court and go for a cup of tea until the hacks had lost the scent.

Dennis wasn't used to dealing with women like my mother. She was in her mid-forties and ten years older than him, for a start. She also, in the words of the song, appeared to him to be an uptown, up-tempo lady, while he felt himself to be more of a downtown, downbeat guy. Up until that moment, he told me, as he worked his way through his second large gin and tonic of the increasingly cool Malagan evening, the women he had usually dealt with in the course of his work had been from a rather different social stratum.

The Street Offences Act of 1959, which was brought in to combat prostitution, meant an awful lot of work for private detectives like Dennis. They had the enviable – or unenviable, depending on your point of view – task of identifying women working as prostitutes so they could be prosecuted by the courts. As essential background work, Dennis was sent out by his boss, the owner of a detective agency on Chancery Lane, to buy a copy of a book called *Sexual Perversions and Anomalies*. This slender but highly informative volume contained material guaranteed to loosen the most clenched jaw. It listed every single activity that prostitutes and their customers might reasonably be expected to partake in. One entire chapter was devoted to men who liked dressing up and what outfits they favoured. 'You know . . . frogmen's gear, stuff like that,' said Dennis. As a reasonably young and avowedly heterosexual single man, he sometimes found himself – how can I put this? – getting a bit more evidence (but only ever of the oral variety) from the alleged prostitutes than he really needed to. What he should have done, of course, was establish beyond all reasonable doubt that they were offering sex for money and then follow the golden rule, i.e. make his excuses and leave. On more than one occasion, however, once he had embarked on the main bit of the investigation, it seems he made his excuses and came. Maybe he got confused. Did he enjoy his work?

'Loved it. Oh yeah, I loved it.'

Nevertheless, for obvious reasons, he wasn't really used to women like my mother.

She was small – just over 5 foot – and voluptuous. Dark medium-length hair, trace of an accent. (When people picked up on it she would tell them she was 'half French, half Spanish', but that wasn't true. She was Jewish. But afraid of anti-Semitism.) Bright, shiny, lively eyes. Vivacious. Ah yes, vivacious. As in: 'Goodness me, young man! Your mother is very vivacious!' Yes, now I remember. When I was small everyone used that word to describe her and it really annoyed me because I never knew what it meant. On a very good day, in the right light and with a following wind, she could look like Gina Lollobrigida, from a distance.

So when Dennis met my mother that day at the High Court, dressed up in the best gear Harrods had to offer, smelling and looking expensive, he thought, he told me, 'Bloody hell. Nice.'

But he also felt he was punching well above his weight. He was renting a flat above a greengrocer's in Reigate: she had a lucrative business running old people's homes and a burgeoning property empire.

'So you were Mellors the gardener and she was Lady Chatterley.'

'You could say that, yeah . . . I suppose so.'

'Mind you . . . look what they ended up doing.'

On D-day (D is for divorce) he ended up following her back home in his car. Just in case. Her suggestion, not his, he said. And then the calls started coming to his boss at the detective agency. Mrs Maitland needed someone to escort her to the bank as she was carrying a lot of money. Could she have Dennis, please? Mrs Maitland was worried that her ex-husband, whom she was going to see to discuss money matters, might get stroppy. One for Dennis, obviously. Mrs Maitland has a problem with rowdy customers. One for you, Den.

Despite the clues and his detective skills, Dennis was slow to catch on. He still didn't think he stood a chance. But then, as in all relationships that eventually go the whole hog, came the Moment When. As in, the Moment When You Just Know It's Going to Happen. In their case, it was a rainy day in Banstead. Dennis was escorting her on yet another contrived job. She needed to make a call but there was a large puddle between her and the telephone box. Without thinking, Dennis lifted her up into his arms and carried her over the puddle and into the phone box. The fuse was lit. No going back now.

He was worried, though. He told her that she was well out of his league. If she went with him, it wouldn't be the Hilton, it would be fish and chips out of the bag. No problem, she said, I might like that.

So, within six months of getting divorced, my mother remarried. She had ended her first union in one room, walked into another and begun her second. The big day was unusually modest by her standards: a quick ceremony at Reigate register office, followed by a couple of drinks at the nearest pub. It was a pity, perhaps, that there wasn't more of a cooling-off period between her marriages. Had she taken a little bit longer – a few weeks, say – she might have foreseen the social, financial and emotional problems that lay ahead. Socially, they came from different worlds. Financially, he was earning 30 quid a week and she was making 30 times that. (This was when the man was supposed to keep the woman, remember.) And emotionally, they went together like a match and a petrol bucket. There was one big area of compatibility, though. Sex. But I'd rather not go there if you don't mind. Not surprisingly, Dennis became uneasy about the way things were panning out. He felt, he said, 'a bit like a ponce, actually: I mean, on my birthday and all that, she bought me a bright yellow E Type Jaguar. On hers, she got flowers.'

The cracks soon coalesced into a fault line. It didn't help that my mother was determined to do a Pygmalion on him. She wanted to control and mould him and nothing would stop her. She informed him: 'You are like a beautiful wild stallion. But that is no fucking good to anyone until it's been broken and made to pull a cart.' Lots of give and take in that relationship, then.

In the first week of the marriage my mother signalled the way things were going to be when she instructed Rosemary, her gap-toothed cockney maid who, it was said, had only one lung, to 'go out with Dennis and buy him some suits . . . money no object'. Overnight, he went from just the one, tatty suit (Man at C & A, thank you very much) to a whole wardrobe full. From Harrods, no less. But he also found himself with a wardrobe full of issues as a result. Identity, pride and all that. He felt uncomfortable: a kept man, a trophy husband. And he couldn't help getting embarrassed when she used to introduce him to her friends and then squeeze his thigh in front of them all and tell them what a good lover he was. He wanted, he said, to curl up and die at moments like that. Truly, this fish was out of water.

I recognized the picture he was painting. I knew she liked getting her own way. But she was generous too. She was always giving away stuff. Expensive stuff. Sometimes I used to wonder how she could afford it. I mean, there wasn't *that* much money in old people's homes, was there? It was always fillet steak, never gammon and pineapple. She didn't understand frugality. Once, early on in their marriage, Dennis had to go out on a surveillance job, which meant sitting in a car for twenty-four hours. She volunteered to make his sandwiches. He opened the hamper expecting to find a round of cheese and pickle and a can of Double Diamond but instead found himself looking at an entire roast chicken, silver cutlery and a bottle of champagne.

But her efforts to control him went further than clothes. She changed his name. Had she taken his, she would have been known as Mrs Warrenner. But she wasn't having that because Dennis had been married once before and so there was already a Mrs Warrenner. So she insisted they take a new name. She decided it was to be Dennis and Bru Wynton. Next up, his job had to go, owing to the inevitable temptations. She didn't want him meeting all those attractive, newly minted single women, fresh out of the divorce courts. Women just like her, in fact. So one minute he was living out his fantasy, investigating dodgy businessmen and sleazy broads, the next he was going down the cash-and-carry clutching a shopping list from my mother. So, yes: there were a lot of problems. And although things were, er, highly satisfactory bedroom-wise, that couldn't keep their fundamentally flawed relationship intact. You might have very nice furniture, but what's the point, if there's something deeply wrong with your house's foundations?

There were thrills and spills on the way, though. Dennis said he found her exciting. Very exciting. Unpredictable. He had never, ever, known anyone like her before. The way she treated people and resolved problems staggered him. Take the case of the Faulty Mercedes. She loved Mercs. She used to shop in them, go on holiday in them and try and kill herself in them. Anyway: one day, one of hers broke down and she sent it to be fixed.

When she went to pick it up, who should she bump into at the Mercedes service garage but Billy 'Wakey Wakey' Cotton, the famous bandleader. He, it transpired, also had a Mercedes that had broken down. Despite the prompt and courteous service she had received – and the fact that the car was now fixed – my mother, just as her car had done, blew a gasket.

'You got Mercedes too?' she said to Wakey Wakey. 'They all bloody fucking shit. They all go wrong, all the time.' This is, and was, of course, a highly defamatory, completely unjustified and irrational thing to say. But once she'd got going she couldn't stop. She went round telling everyone who was there – i.e. unsuspecting and startled Mercedes customers – much the same thing. A couple of days later Mercedes informed her they were suing her for slander in the High Court.

But she was good on the law, I seem to remember. So what Dennis told me next came as no surprise. Her lawyer, the flamboyant and very tall Humphrey Benson, quite rightly argued that she didn't have a leg to stand on. He advised her to admit her guilt and make a small offer of damages as a gesture so the whole thing would go away. But she was adamant. She wanted to fight. And she had a plan. She sent an appallingly badly written letter, in pencil, to Mercedes' very expensive firm of lawyers in Mayfair. It went something like:

Dear Mr Mercedes

I got your letter what you wrote yesterday. Have I got to come to yore court? I don't trust you bastards.
Anyway I got to sit near the door coz I am nervous and I have to keep going to the loo. And will I have to wear a wig? Cos I am representing myself, know what I mean?
Thank you
Mrs Wynton

The lawyers sent a suitably snotty letter back ('We have received your letter, which was apparently intended as a reply. We have decided it is not in our best interests to communicate with you directly in the future. Please supply us with the name of your legal counsel . . .'). Oops. Bad move. That only egged her on even more.

Dear Mr Mercedes
  You fucking right upset me now. So I ain't gonna write
to you any more, ever.
  Thank You
  Mrs Wynton

This was fun. Every time Mr Mercedes replied, my mother would fire off another beauty. Eventually, the two sides met before a judge in chambers at the High Court to decide whether the case should proceed. By this time, however, Mercedes had realized what they were up against. Wisely, they decided there was no point in carrying on. First, given my mother's form, they knew that if the case was heard in open court, it would be a very high-risk strategy indeed, the legal equivalent of juggling with chainsaws. Second, it wouldn't make for good publicity: 'Mercedes sues middle-aged woman from Surrey' and all that. So they waved the white flag. All they wanted, they said to the judge in chambers, was for my mother to apologize and pay her share of the costs. Like, yeah. She argued that since it was Mercedes who wanted to sue her, they should pay the costs. She wanted her day in court but now they were trying to call it off. What sort of behaviour is that? she argued. The judge bought it. Mercedes lost 5–0. They got no apology and paid all the costs. Humphrey Benson, a professional solicitor, remember, was staggered. A small, irrational Jewish woman who didn't even speak English until she was sixteen had committed an appalling slander against one of the biggest and richest multinationals in the world, and it was they who had ended up on the canvas, begging for mercy. Not bad.

Garages often ended up in the firing line, said Dennis. The next company to cop it after Mercedes was another very well-known firm of British car manufacturers. Their local dealership sold her a car that went wrong. As far as she was concerned they were to blame. But they wouldn't pick up the bill for the repairs. So she went nuclear. She parked the said (all white) car in a lay-by right opposite the dealership and painted slogans all over it in bright green paint. Slogans like: 'THESE CARS ARE SHIT! DON'T BUY THEM.'

It's funny, I said to Dennis. twenty-five years after her one-woman campaigns I unwittingly employed similar, but less spectacular, tactics as a reporter on the BBC's consumer pro-gramme, *Watchdog*. He knew, he said: he'd seen me on telly and thought the same thing himself. Once we did a story about the (supposedly) poor service provided by Parcel Force, the delivery firm. I suggested a subtle redesign of their logo: why not change the 'o' in the company's name to an 'a'? We then filmed a load of their newly logoed vans driving up and down the street, getting lost. Cheap and juvenile, I know, but strangely satisfying.

It was fine when Dennis and Bru were united against a common enemy. But when they turned on each other, it wasn't. Not for her *The Buddhist Guide to Conflict Resolution*. When it came to arguments she played for very high stakes. She much preferred the forty-two-sleeping-pill overdose to soothing words at bedtime. Dennis remembered having to fish her out of Accident and Emergency, post-overdose, on more than one occa-sion. There was, for her, simply no such thing as an idle threat.

Occasionally she would eschew self-harm for other, more cre-ative methods of winning the argument. Throwing Dennis's entire possessions out of a first-floor window on to the driveway below was a favourite. As was, humiliatingly for him, her tactic of calling the police and telling them to escort him off the prem-ises. The poor bloke would then have to take one of the officers aside and gently explain that they were married, he lived there, that he used to be a policeman too, you know, and that no, he wasn't a wife-beater/drunk/madman.

Cars, as you may also have gathered, featured heavily in their relationship. When she wasn't buying him one, threatening to drive off a cliff in one or headed for the High Court over one, she would be using one to make a point, forcefully. Once, she decided that Dennis was spending too long at his favourite haunt, the Down the Queen Vic. She, unbeknown to him, was growing increasingly frustrated at his absences. So there he was, sat at the table, having a quiet early evening pint with some mates, when the pub door flew open and the whole place – in the style of a cheesy western – suddenly went horribly quiet. Except it wasn't Yul Brynner, all dressed in black, in a saloon in the Midwest. It was the Queen Vic in North Cheam, and it was 'your missus, Dennis . . . and she's in her nightie'.

She strode over to his table and, without saying a word, knocked every single drink on it flying. And out she went. But it wasn't over yet. Just after Dennis had finished making his excuses and was starting to leave, he heard noises coming from outside the pub. Crash! Bang! Boof! noises. And, curiously, revving engine noises. When he got outside, he found her smashing her little green mini (her reserve car) into his Mercedes, repeatedly. She was ramming her vehicle into his from two or three yards away, reversing and then repeating the medicine. As I say, Gandhi was not a role model.

The violence wasn't limited to cars either. I don't remember too much about your relationship with her, I told Dennis, but I do have a mental image in my mind: a stabbing incident of some kind. But I can't remember who was stabbing who. Such are the happy memories of my childhood. He enlightened me. 'We had a row about something. And she told me to fuck off and get out of her house. But I couldn't, could I? Anyway, I happened to have a knife in my hands . . .'

'As you do.'

'As you do. Actually, it was because she was threatening to drive off somewhere and I wanted to stop her. She threatened to run me over if I stood in the way, so I'd got a knife, so I could puncture her tyres, to stop her going. She saw the knife and said, 'You want to kill me, don't you?' And I said, 'No I don't.' And she said, 'Yes you do.' And I said, 'No I don't, I'd kill meself before I'd do that.' And to prove it, I turned the knife inwards, so it was pointing at me stomach. And she said, 'Go on, then,' and gave my hand a shove, and in it went. I didn't think it had gone in deep, but it had . . . then she said she was going to call the police and I thought, oh God, no, not again, so I drove off. After a while it started to really hurt and I realized there was blood, like, pumping out of me, and it was all over my shirt and the car and everything. So when I got to Mitcham it was really fucking hurting, so I just patched it up myself. I didn't want to go to hospital and all that, and explain it, 'cos it would have been embarrassing. Pity, really . . . 'cos me intestine got inflamed, and started poking through the hole in my stomach where the knife went in. I had to have an operation to put it right. Look . . .'

Dennis lifted up the front of his shirt and pointed to a neat, 2-inch-wide pink slit. That reminds me of a complete nutter I used to go out with, I told Dennis. She really used to scare me. Once, she brought a noisy, sociable cricket tea to a momentary, embarrassed standstill by waving a carving knife in the air and noisily proclaiming, in her shrill American accent: 'They're right, you know! The best way to a man's heart really is through his stomach . . . with a knife!'

These domestic traumas were, fittingly, taking place against a background of international violence. The Middle East was in turmoil, and Israel was having to defend herself against her neighbours. During a rare moment of calm between them, Dennis found himself experiencing an intense and newly found loyalty to Israel, given that it was the country of my mother's birth. So he turned up at their embassy in London and volunteered for duty. They thanked him but turned him down. I can't help thinking he would have been safer if he had been accepted for duty out there.

Even when they were apart, the psychological game-playing/torture continued. Once, Dennis told me – with a smile, I noticed – he'd been slung out by her and had gone back to his bedsit above the greengrocer's in Reigate. One afternoon she got one of his mates to go and see him, under the pretence of delivering a parcel. Dennis noticed immediately that his mate was wearing one of the suits she had bought for him during their honeymoon period. A bit sinister, wasn't it? I said to Dennis. He just laughed. You had to be there, I guess.

You don't have to be a marriage guidance counsellor to work out that Dennis and my mother's union was as solid as a chocolate fireguard. Within months she started going on about what a terrible mistake she'd made marrying him in the first place. After two years, the minimum period that had to elapse in those days before the marriage could end, they got divorced.

Gutted, traumatized and shell-shocked – his words, not mine – Dennis at least thought he'd escaped from her and it all. With no home and no job to go to he ended up on a building site in Bournemouth run by George, a mate of his. But she wasn't done with him yet. The legal ties may have been broken but not the emotional ones. She started leaving messages for him at the building site. George, thinking he knew what was good for Dennis, never passed any on. One day the inevitable happened and Dennis answered the phone himself.

'Where are you, you bastard?' she said. 'Where have you been? Come back. I need you.'

And so the whole mad, crazy, destructive cycle began again.

'Is it – er – fair to say that she had . . . a bit of a hold on you, then?' I ventured, stirring the last remnants of the ice into my Diet Pepsi. Call me Sherlock!

'Oh yeah. Yeah.'

He paused and stared into his drink, his fourth of the evening.

'Let's be frank about it. I'd burned all my bridges for her. I gave everything up for her. Sure, there were other women. But she was . . . different from them. There was this excitement and challenge about her. And when she called, I would just go back to her, like a little dog, feeling sorry for myself.'

There were also, of course, good practical reasons for going back. Let's face it: if you're doing back-breaking, poorly paid work on a building site in Bournemouth and your ex-wife, who still has a hold on you, tells you she needs you, and that there will be money, suits, expensive bedlinen and fillet steaks for dinner, you've got to be tempted, haven't you?

So, unbelievably, North Cheam's very own Richard Burton and Elizabeth Taylor decided to give marriage another go. This time, though, Dennis thought it might be wise to lay down a few ground rules. A verbal pre-nuptial agreement. By now he'd started working as a private detective again and things were going well. They both agreed therefore that it would be a good idea for Dennis, his self-respect and their relationship if he didn't resume cash-and-carry-type duties. I was there for ceremony number two, which, for some reason, took place at a register office in Jersey. Dennis and I played football on the beach at St Brelade's Bay afterwards, to celebrate. You know what's coming next.

Sure, they were happy. For a while. But then it came to pass that on the fourth day of their marriage, literally, she rang him at work and said: 'This isn't working: I want you to stop doing your job and come and help me with the business.'

He refused. That was that. The marriage hadn't lasted a week. Dennis had no regrets: if he had gone back to working with her, or rather for her, he knew perfectly well how it would have ended up. And he was probably 100 per cent right, if it's possible to be such a thing.

He moved into his bachelor-pad bedsit above the greengrocer's shop in Reigate again and resumed his daily attendance sessions at the Down the Queen Vic. He met Sue. She pulled pints, he pulled her. They moved in together and even managed to survive unscheduled visits from You Know Who. On one occasion, Sue answered the door, only to be brushed aside by my mother doing an impression of a front-row forward with the ball under her arm, headed for the try line. My mother's opening line was: 'Get out of the way. You are just his tart. It is I who am his wife.'

Soon, however, the surprise visits subsided. My mother then went through her Every Breath You Take phase. Every so often, Dennis, the professional surveillance expert, would find himself the subject of an attempted surveillance operation, carried out by a strange woman in a green Mini. She wasn't as good as she might have been, however. Dennis lived near the end of a cul-de-sac, so once she had driven past his window, peering ostentatiously out of her car, she would then have to turn around. This involved her executing a very poor and very noisy three-point turn. Sue, Dennis's girlfriend, saw the funny side. In fact, reader, she married him. And that's her now, thirty-odd years on, coming out of the bedroom, rubbing her eyes, asking us whether we want a cup of tea. No thanks, Sue, we're going to bed.

Just before we retired for the night I asked Dennis what he felt whenever he thought of my mother. 'I loved her,' he said. 'I really, really loved her.'

On the way to my room I saw a familiar photograph on the

wall. It was Dennis as a young man on a horse, when he was in the Household Cavalry. Very impressive. Just as I remembered it. Helmet, knee-length black leather boots, tight white trousers, sword – the lot.

'Aha. That photograph,' I said. 'Last time I saw that, it was behind the washing machine at Egmont Road.'

'What?'

I checked myself.

'Er, nothing. What time do you get up in the morning?'

The next day we played golf. Dennis was pretty handy. Especially for a 72-year-old who'd had stomach and bowel cancer. I was surprised he could play at all, let alone whack the ball as far as he did. But then anyone who can survive my mother, I thought, can survive pretty much anything.

There were more bones to pick over so we talked as we walked. We replayed some of their rows: he put on the mental CD labelled *Now That's What I Call Arguing, Volume 3*. An early humdinger was over the way she treated some of the old people in her care, he said. My ears pricked up. According to Dennis, my mother decided to move an old man who'd been living in Twin Gables, the old people's home that doubled as the family home, even though he'd been in the same room for years. She thought she could get more money for it so she let it to someone else. But the old boy had grown accustomed to her place: he had pictures of his family up on the wall and not surprisingly he didn't want to move. But my mother insisted. The old boy was in tears but it made no difference. Dennis protested. It still made no difference. She told him, in fact, to 'fuck off and mind his own business'. Did he take it any farther?

'Nah. There was no point. No one could stop her doing what she wanted to do.'

This was bad. But not terrible. And not, presumably, what my friend the hack with a face like rare roast beef was referring to. But it was one of the reasons – the main one, in fact – why I was here.

'The old people's homes. What happened there? Why did she close them down and suddenly start running hotels?'

'Oh, yeah. I only found out about this later. There was some dodgy stuff going on there, I think. I'm not sure but I think she might have had her licence taken away by the local council.'

'Dodgy? How dodgy?'

'Well, there were a few disgruntled people, I remember. I only found out about it after it all happened. Your mother blamed your father, actually, she said he was behind it all. There was some stuff about it in the papers, I think. And there was a lot of correspondence taking place.'

'Yes, but . . . how dodgy are we talking?'

'Er . . . low-level embezzlement, I think. That kind of thing.'

'We're not talking Robert Maxwell, are we?'

'I don't think so . . . no.'

27 March 2005

It hasn't been a good week. Today is my forty-fourth birthday and I've got a bad case of the triple Fs: Fat, Forty and Feeling it. What's happened? I used to be young once. Now I'm not. When did that happen?

It's not been a great week for investigative journalism either. First off, I had to interview the saucer-eyed Tessa Jowell, the Quite Important Minister in charge of the Department for Culture, Media and Sport. The general consensus at *Tonight with Trevor McDonald* is that it was one of the worst interviews ever conducted in the history of space and time. I disagree. It was worse than that. The problem was ... well, the problem was me, actually. I just sat there like a sack of potatoes while she went on about what a great idea twenty-four-hour drinking was. My job was to interrupt her, challenge her and get some sparks flying on screen. Having seen the rushes, however, I know that the only things flying when this interview gets shown will be viewers – out of the room.

In mitigation, Tessa Jowell did her I'm-a-nice-person-so-be gentle-with-me trick, which I fell for. She recognized me from the last time I had interviewed her – or she pretended to, at any rate – and asked how I was. She also asked my opinion on something or other and enquired whether we all wanted tea. By the time the interview came round and the cameras started running, instead of being a lean, hungry, sharp Rottweiler, I was a simpering, pathetic puppy. I mean, how can I be all confident and gladiatorial with someone who's just given me a cup of tea? Third, and most importantly, my mind wasn't really on the job. Minutes before the interview started, when I should have been studying my notes and memorizing arcane statistics on the effects of longer pub hours, I made a call on my mobile to my not-very-good friend, aka the hack with the roast beef complexion.

ME: 'Hi, is that Peter?'

HACK WTRBC: 'Who's this?'

ME: 'Jonny . . . Jonathan Maitland. Jonathan. You know, Epsom, old people's homes thirty years ago and all that stuff.'

HACK WTRBC: 'Yes? And?'

ME: 'Look, can you help me? It's just that I'm at that time, you know, when you want to know more about what's gone on in your life, and I just wanted to know about what went on.'

HACK WTRBC: 'Look, I don't want to be rude but I'm busy and I haven't got time to be your researcher. I'm sure you can find out for yourself. You could start at the local library, for one thing. OK? Goodbye.'

That's why my interview with Tessa Jowell was rubbish. When, for example, she said 'These proposals are all about making life easier and more enjoyable for the vast majority of the population,' I should have been thinking, 'Right. Interrupt her when she next draws breath with the results of our Exclusive *Tonight* Poll which shows that a lot of people disagree with her.' But instead I found myself thinking: 'God. Sutton and Cheam Library. Sutton and Cheam Library. Good cake. When was I last there? The late seventies. Jill Skinner! My first girlfriend, Jill Skinner, who liked Genesis! I used to meet her there! Is it still open? I wonder. And do they have a local newspaper section? And how far does it go back?' By which time the minister had stopped talking. Even though she had been talking for quite a long time, non-stop. And she was looking at me. And she hadn't said anything for three seconds. Her handler/spin doctor didn't need telling.

'Right, great, I think that's enough. Thanks for the interview, the minister needs to be somewhere else now. You've got all you need and so have we. Thanks.'

My producer gave me a dirty look. I couldn't blame him.

One day in the summer of 1975

'Hey . . . is this your mother?'

The boy at the desk next to mine, Simon Rhodes, was keeping his voice down and quite right too. We were in the back row of the classroom and just about to take our end-of-year French exam. The teacher was handing out the papers a few yards away from us, out of earshot. Simon had something on his lap and was pointing to it. I couldn't see what it was but his demeanour suggested it was interesting. This wasn't the time or place I thought, but who cares. After making sure the teacher was at a safe distance I leant across.

'This was on the front page . . .' he whispered, as it slipped from his grasp to mine. '. . . isn't it your mum?' It was a sheet of newsprint that had been torn from a local newspaper.

'The exam will begin in two minutes,' said a voice. 'You may not, I repeat not, look at your papers until then.'

Nothing was going to stop me looking at mine. I pushed myself back from my desk, my chair scrunching on the floor. I laid the page out on my lap and took as much in as I could. There was a picture of a woman in front of a familiar-looking house. And a banner headline that read something like:

'WOMAN WITH SIX MONTHS TO LIVE OPENS HOMOSEXUAL HOTEL IN EWELL'.

I couldn't work out how it was relevant to me. And I was tense because the exam was starting any second. But then I noticed that the woman in the picture was my mother. What was going on? Then there was a bit about a woman with cancer who had been told by doctors that she was going to die. And she was opening Britain's first hotel for gays, and local residents were up in arms about it. The woman was my mother, it said. How so? I didn't know anything about this. It didn't make any sense. Not then. Not in Class U4B, just before the end-of-year French exam. I was baffled. Disoriented. There seemed to be two options: exit stage left, quickly, and run. Or stay and get to grips with the difference between the perfect and pluperfect tenses of *avoir*. It didn't feel right to make a fuss so I went for the *avoir* option. Yes, there were things to think about. But those things, the things I had just read, and the implications of them, had no real significance to me at that moment. Maybe I had gone into mild shock. They were just words on a thin bit of paper after all. And maybe it was a kind of strange, perverse joke.

Suddenly Mrs Lane, my housemaster's wife, was standing at the entrance to the classroom. She was trying to get the teacher's attention. She got mine instead, and as she did so she gave me a look, one that I now know means 'Are you all right?' All I could think of was that there was a French essay to write. Mrs Lane went straight up to the teacher and said something quietly to him, glancing at me as she did so. She then came over and told me, quietly, to go with her. Some of the boys turned round to see what was going on. It was a bit embarrassing. Right in the middle of a French exam.

I had never been in Mrs Lane's lounge before. The house she shared with her husband was part of the huge Victorian building where I and fifty-five other boys aged between thirteen and eighteen spent every night of the week. Our bit of the building, the bit where the fifty-five boys lived, had the same dank, soulless, Dickensian atmosphere that all mid-seventies boarding schools had: no love, bare concrete floors, wrought-iron banisters, cheap straw mattresses and ugly shower chambers that echoed lots. The Lanes' lounge, though, was another world. Here there were cushions, patterned carpets, deep sofas, warmth. Our bit of the house smelt of pumice stones and metal. This bit was all warm radiators and tea. And Mrs Lane. She walked in with a plate of cakes and a copy of the offending newspaper under her arm.

I can't remember exactly what Mrs Lane said but I can remember how it sounded. Soothing. I remember how it felt too. Good. I enjoyed the attention. A warm, attractive woman with breasts . . . breasts! . . . was sitting, er, really close to me on the sofa, so close that I could feel her next to me. Thank you, God. But then something started to happen. Words from the front page of the paper, which was laid out on the table in front of us, began to permeate my brain. I can't remember exactly what they said, but I can remember how they felt when they began to make sense. All that stuff about 'cancer' and 'six months to live'.

Trouble was, I wasn't sure whether it was true or not. It was just words on paper, wasn't it? But . . . maybe it was true.

I mean, if it was in the newspapers, it must be. Oh God.

I felt as if I had been cut adrift. I didn't know what was going on.

18 June 2005

I am not, as you may have gathered, an only child. I have two older brothers (Peter and Maurice) and a sister (Rachel), who are all in their fifties. So why, you might be asking, haven't I tried finding out from them what happened? Well, it's not quite as simple as that. Our family, I am afraid, is a bit fucked up. There are more feuds going on than in a Mafia convention. I don't speak to Rachel or Maurice. And Peter doesn't speak to them much, either. Oh – and Maurice doesn't speak to Rachel. It's very easy to forget who's feuding with whom, in fact. As a result I sometimes get confused and stop speaking to myself. So I can't just ring Maurice or Rachel out of the blue and start firing questions at them. There are years of silence and several walls of misunderstanding and mistrust to break down first.

Maybe it's something we inherited from our mother: she always seemed to have fallen out with one relative or other. It used to get pretty vicious and would often last a very long time. So I guess I was only carrying on a venerable family tradition when all communication with Maurice ceased a couple of years ago after a flurry of unpleasant e-mails passed between us. Before I knew it, a playground spat had turned into a nuclear war and so by the end of the correspondence I got a message from him along the lines of 'Leave us alone, we never want to see you again'. Blimey. How did that happen?

Anyway, I've been thinking about this episode – which surprised me, in that it upset me much more than I thought it would – a lot, recently. How can I write a book about what my mother did or didn't get up to back in the sixties, without asking Maurice? Pete never gave much attention to anything that went on. He was too busy playing in a band and sleeping until two in the afternoon. But Maurice, a highly intelligent linguistics expert and qualified barrister, always took an interest. And he always had an eye for detail.

So here goes.

From: jmaitland@xxxxx
To: Mmaitland @xxxxxx
Sent: June 18 2005
Subject: feud for thought

Dear Maurice

I know we're not supposed to be talking to each other but something has come up which I know will interest you greatly and I thought you might appreciate the chance to contribute. I am writing a book about our mother, following on from an incident involving a reporter who worked on local papers in Epsom in the 60s. He intimated to me that she was involved in something pretty dodgy when she used to run the old people's homes, but he wouldn't say exactly what it was. And he's not being very cooperative either. Everyone always said I should write a book about her, so that's what I'm doing. It's just that this has come up along the way, so I want to get to the bottom of it. I wondered if you had any clues or information? And please let's not let it degenerate into a slanging match again as I found the last outbreak of hostilities distressing. If you don't want to reply I quite understand. I really hope you and your family are doing well.

All the best

Jonny

PS: I got married last year.

That still leaves Rachel, of course. That's a tricky one. I'll come back to that another time. That's quite enough trawling through emotionally shark-infested waters for one day, I think. There is also work to do. The people on *House of Horrors*, the show I do about dodgy traders and conmen, have come up with a good idea. They want to do something different for the new series. Instead of me spending weeks on end watching and listening to secretly filmed camera footage of plumbers and roofers ripping people off, the plan is for me to actually do some ripping off myself. I am supposed to be getting lessons in how to be a successful high-pressure salesman from the UK's leading exponent of it – a bloke called Jay – and then putting what I've learned into practice. Once I've absorbed the tricks of the trade I will be sent out and secretly filmed trying to persuade bored housewives and old codgers to part with thousands of pounds for rubbish products that they don't really need. I will only be pretending, of course, but hopefully it will make above-average TV. The first lesson is next week and I am looking forward to it.

1972–75

I don't know how deeply my mother's disastrous double marriage and double divorce to Dennis affected her because we never really talked about it. In fact we never talked about anything very much. That was because, just as in previous years, I hardly ever saw her. She was always 'busy with the business, darling. I am doing it for you, you know, my little darling, for your future . . .' Occasionally, however, she would enter a room where I happened to be, look glamorous, order minions around, and then proceed to make an almighty fuss of me for a few seconds. But just occasionally, the subject of Dennis would come up. In which case the volcanic flow of motherly love that had temporarily enveloped me would abruptly cease, to be replaced with a torrent of spectacular-sounding foul-mouthed vitriol, along the lines of: 'He is a fucking bastard. He let me down. He better be happy with his fucking barmaid tart, he no gonna get me back.' But then attack always was her best form of defence. Even at that young age, though, I felt protective towards her. I think I must have sensed that she had been hurt by the whole thing.

Another reason why we didn't see much of each other was

because she was one of those people who thought there were few better things you could do for your children than to give them a good, old-fashioned, British private-school education. She had always been deeply impressed by things and people that she considered to be intrinsically, genuinely British. In fact that's why my surname is the one I have now. By rights, it should be Melman. That's what my father was called when she married him. But she was always worried about anti-Semitism and thought Melman sounded too Jewish. So one day, when an ex-British Army major called Maitland came to stay at one of the old people's homes and impressed her with his manners, bearing and general all-round Britishness, she decided to nick his surname in the hope that some of what he had would rub off on us. She also found herself very taken by a guest who told her that he had sent all of his children to a prep school, a damn fine place in the heart of the Surrey countryside. If it was good enough for him, etc., etc. . . .

That meant me being left for nine months of the year in a scary-looking building on top of a hill in the middle of England's green and pleasant land. It felt like I had been jettisoned in the middle of nowhere. I literally had no idea where I was. I later learned that I was in fact not far from Cranleigh in Surrey. Once a term, if I was lucky, my mother would visit. She would sweep up the long, steep driveway in whatever Mercedes she happened to be driving that month and take me for tea and cake (make that cakes) at a local hotel.

At first I used to dread being left at that place. The worst bit was always the first night of a new term. There were several dormitories, all of them named after cathedrals, in which anything up to thirty boys slept. For some reason all the new boys slept in one called Norwich. I remember my first-ever night there. I was bemused, bereft and scared. (A bit like when I visit Norwich now, in fact.) The beds in all the 'dorms' were made of cold black metal and had straw mattresses that sank in the middle. Talking after lights-out was strictly forbidden but sometimes we'd chance our arms with a few ghost stories, which only served to ratchet up the reading on the grimometer even more. There wasn't a lot of love around. Nearly all the teachers were male and, as befits an institution of that sort, when it came to sexual matters, one or two liked going off the beaten track somewhat. The science teacher, who has long since gone to the great lab in the sky, used to have out-of-control eyebrows (nothing pervy about that, I know, but be patient) and claimed to have invented a machine that could circumcise little boys. This, of course, meant that he had to spend hours researching the subject in order to perfect his invention. (I saw it once – it looked like a small bell on the end of the handle of a teaspoon.) This 'research' involved heavily super-vised shower sessions and, during our uncannily regular weighing sessions, him sitting on a chair which meant that his face was never more than 6 inches away from the acorns of his desire. And there were floggings. I got one for forgetting a temporary edict that all meals were to be eaten in silence. The moment we sat down after grace I asked a boy next to me whether I could have his sausage. He wouldn't reply so I kept asking. Thirty seconds later I was getting six strokes with the slipper on my bare and very substantial 12-year-old arse. After the initial shock of board-ing school, however, I became anaesthetized to the grimness of it all. Little things helped: although there wasn't very much empa-thy in the air, there were enough females – a couple of matrons – to gawp at and fantasize about and thus prevent mass outbreaks of uncontrolled homosexuality. And there was music. We were allowed radios. Which meant listening to Radio One's chart run-down every Sunday afternoon to see how T Rex, David Bowie, Slade, Mud and the Rubettes et al. were doing.

Because it was a typically British prep school of its time, the food was indescribably shit. The stuff you got given for breakfast, which was billed as 'porridge', was particularly and memorably brutal. It was grey, cold and lumpy and was like bile mixed with cement powder. As a result, I lived for other boys' birthdays as that meant we were allowed – praise the Lord, hallelujah, pass the prayer mat – cake. Real, yummy cake. Supplied not by the school, mind you, but by the parents of whoever happened to be celebrating that day. But there was a catch. Not everyone in the school got a slice. It was up to the Birthday Boy to decide who was going to be on his 'cake list'. After some deeply upsetting days, when the cake trays would pass agonizingly by, never to return, I realized it was time to develop some lobbying skills. So I got pretty good at identifying and sucking up to imminent Birthday Boys. This, at last, was one area of parenting where my mother excelled. My birthday cakes got bigger and more extravagant every year. She once sent a minion to the school with a car dragging along a trailer carrying a strawberry and cream chocolate sponge the size of Stonehenge. I'm surprised she didn't apply for planning permission before she got it made. Come cake time, it felt good to be popular.

The alternative to being holed up in the Surrey countryside's version of Colditz would have been to stay at home and be a day boy at a local school. But I'm not sure how preferable that would have been. For a start, I wasn't quite sure where home was. Because it was around this time that my mother announced she had invested in yet another business. A large country hotel in Bosham in Sussex, just on the outskirts of Chichester. Looking back on it, with the aid of a large portion of cod psychology, it may be that the Bosham Hotel was a diversionary tactic, i.e. one to divert her attention away from the ten-car motorway pile-up that her relationship with Dennis had turned into. Whatever: the end result was that now, with a second hotel for her to run, I had two homes and saw even less of her than before. And that was saying something. So Colditz-on-the-Hill did, at least, provide essential ingredients that my childhood would otherwise have lacked: a routine, discipline, stability and predictability.

She was very much in charge at both hotels and therefore, by the nature of her position and her personality, Always and Irrefutably and Uncannily Right. So there were very few people, if any, prepared to say 'no' to her. If she wanted something she usually got it. No matter how outlandish or seemingly off beam. Hence the strange affair – literally – of Edward.

He was the first man my mother – ahem – 'investigated', in the Years after Dennis. Edward was a grey-haired, baby-faced, middle-aged waiter with a kindly smile who looked a bit like Liberace. But that wasn't all he and Mr L. had in common. Edward was a rampant queen. And somewhere on the gay grapevine he had heard about this unusual woman and her unusual establishment and realized there was work and fun to be had. But the fun he ended up getting wasn't quite the sort he had expected. Within weeks of taking a job at the Nonsuch Park Hotel, and soon after my mother's second and final split from Dennis, Edward found himself on more than just his employer's payroll. They became lovers. True to form, my mother did her Pygmalion bit and kitted him out in a whole new wardrobe from Harrods. Silk shirts, designer suits, the lot. It didn't shock me: it just seemed par for the course with her. This, for me, was normality. One day I had a stepfather, the next his place had been taken by a gay middle-aged waiter from Coventry. I didn't know much about sex at the time but I did know enough to be aware that, as far as Edward was concerned, this was a bit odd – the sexual equivalent of a lifelong communist suddenly taking a job as a stockbroker. But my mother was very liberated when it

came to sex so questions from me about this unorthodox relationship were not only allowed but welcomed and answered
head-on. So, I asked her one day, 'Mum . . . how can you have
sex with Edward, if he's gay?'

'Aha!' she replied. 'There are . . . there are ways and means of
turning on a man.'

'Really? What are they?'

She then explained, in sufficient detail to make me wish I'd
never asked in the first place.

Her relationship with Edward didn't last long, however,
mainly because his, er, 'nature' reasserted itself once too often
for my mother's liking. As a result my mother suffered the indignity of having to be treated for an unfortunate condition at the
St Helier hospital's Special Clinic. After a while it became apparent that Edward had decamped, but not literally. To Coventry.
From whence he came. He may have been hastened along that
path, I suspect, after an incident involving Dennis. In a nutshell,
the latter poured hot tea over the former after finding him in bed
one afternoon with my mother. Dennis and she may have been
separated by this time – he had only come back to collect some
belongings – but he still found himself acting on spur-of-the-
moment jealousy. So: afternoon trysts with a gay waiter
followed by a tea-based assault, on said waiter, by your outraged
private detective ex-husband: just another average day for her,
then.

Not surprisingly, my mother's lifestyle had a not altogether
beneficial effect on the service she was able to provide to her
guests. One of the few mementoes I have kept from that time is
a letter from a disgruntled and slightly bewildered customer of
the Nonsuch Park Hotel who wrote to complain to the British
Tourist Board (BTB). They sent a copy of it on to my mother,
although I'm not sure she ever read it. The writer described the

scene that met him on his first night there, thus: 'There was a small, neurotic woman with dyed hair racing, in a pink night-dress, around the Nonsuch Hotel reception night and day, screaming abuse at a domestic called Rosemary and locked in constant and violent arguments with her husband, a man called Dennis.' As result, the BTB informed my mother, the Nonsuch was being dropped from their official hotel guide. I don't think she was too bothered.

Once Edward was off the scene I recall another employee, called Dominic, taking his place, albeit briefly. This one was a lot younger than my mother – late twenties, I think – and looked a bit like a footballer. Dark hair, snake hips, winning smile. Once he'd got the Suitcase Treatment, however, i.e. the trunk packed full of expensive new gear from fashionable London department stores, he was off. Not surprisingly, I think my mother got the feeling that she'd been taken advantage of and so alliances of that kind ceased for a few years.

It wasn't as if she didn't have plenty of other things to occupy her. Two hotels, more than 60 miles apart, each requiring round-the-clock supervision from her, or someone she could trust. But the problem, apparently, was that there just weren't that many people she felt she could trust. I don't know why. There had been my father, of course – he, from what she used to say at the time, could be guaranteed to do whatever she asked of him. But Dennis, as she had discovered, wasn't really suited to the cater-ing game. And once he'd gone, that left Rosie, the one-lunged, gap-toothed cockney maid, who had been around for years and was instinctively and unswervingly loyal. But she wasn't by any means what you'd call management material. Rosie may have had many qualities but running a medium-sized guest house wasn't one of them. For a start, she came from a poor, working-class area of west London and so through no fault of her own wasn't what you would call 'strong' on the basics of reading, writing and arithmetic. The latter being particularly important if you are trying to work out why your bar is losing several hundred pounds a week, even though it's full to the brim with customers most of the time. So: while Rosie the Unready was left, on her own, to run the Nonsuch Park Hotel, my mother concentrated all her firepower on the Bosham, in Chichester. That wasn't easy either.

The catering business, you see, has always attracted its fair share of rogues, charlatans and chancers. East European chefs who like loading their Ladas and larders with lobsters nicked from the hotel kitchen. Light-fingered bar staff and alcoholic waiters. That sort of thing. And my mother's business in Bosham was no different. When I went to see Dennis in Malaga he said he couldn't believe how brazen some of the employees were when it came to ripping her off. Some of the staff might as well have turned up for work with masks and hooped T-shirts with bags marked 'swag' on their backs. Soon, it became clear that both her hotels were haemorrhaging money. To make things worse, my mother had no money management skills whatsoever. Her instinctive response to an overdraft, curiously, was always to try to spend her way out of it. One day, soon after receiving a letter warning of impending financial doom from her bank manager, she ordered several ornate marble Greek statues to be shipped in from Athens, at a cost of several thousand pounds.

Then came the double whammy to add to this already highly unsatisfactory state of business affairs: my mother's apparent incurable illness and the economic recession. It was the mid-seventies, remember, and there was an oil crisis. The stock market was in the middle of losing three-quarters of its value and there was unemployment, raging inflation and no one had any money to spend. The three-day week imposed by the Heath government had rendered the Bosham Hotel cold, dark and empty half the time, leaving its staff to wander, bewildered, around the town. These three things, then – a lack of decent, qualified staff, the recession and her health – had the same effect, eventually, on her businesses as a high wind on a pack of cards.

Ah yes. Her health. I can quite understand if you think I'm coming over as rather callous on that score. But in my defence, it was hard to know what was really going on. Did she have cancer or not? I wasn't sure. Lots of other people seemed to think so, I know that. I got used to them tutting a lot and the look of pity in their eyes when she used to talk about it in front of them, which she did often. I found the whole thing rather perplexing. That deathbed business – 'The money . . . is in the bottom drawer', etc., etc. – and the similar incidents that followed may have knocked the empathetic stuffing out of me, I fear, so I wasn't as concerned or upset as I perhaps should have been. I mean, I really did think she had died, that day. So after that, emotionally, there weren't many places to go. It was still a shock, nevertheless, to read in the local paper soon after that about her not having long to live. Maybe, I figured, the deathbed scene was kind of, like, a dress rehearsal for the real thing, which would be along in a few months. But when, after a few months, she still seemed to be as hale and hearty as ever, I felt a little bit . . . let down. Sounds terrible, I know. But after a while, I felt as if my emotions were being manipulated a bit. Then again, she *was* ill, I knew that. Because I used to visit her in hospital around this time, and she would look very rough indeed and have tubes and stuff sticking out of her. Confusing or what? Her demise, quite possibly, might have been every bit as imminent as she made out. But the time line, I couldn't help noticing, kept slipping. It was a new form of the disease: renewable-lease cancer. She would say she had six months to live. But then six months later, she would say it again. When that six months was up, she'd start saying it again. And so on.

It was around this time that she started using her illness as a weapon, or diversionary tactic. And very effective it was too. If she was in an argument that she feared she was losing, she would often bung in the comment – in the manner of a terrorist lobbing a grenade into a crowded bar – that she had six months to live, and was 'a dying woman'. This was a great tactic, of course, as it couldn't be trumped. Whoever was on the receiving end – a customer, complaining about a room, or a frustrated local tradesman wanting to be paid – would naturally back down immediately. Cue ashen face and mumbled, embarrassed apologies.

Anyway: all this added up to a pretty unfortunate equation, which could be stated thus: illness + recession + no one to run her businesses properly in her absences = financial ruin. I don't remember the exact day it all came tumbling down. But I can recall the after-effects. One day, the Nonsuch Park Hotel was thriving and full of customers. The next – to a loud chorus of whispers from the staff about things like 'bankruptcy' and 'repossession', things I hadn't a clue about, although they sounded suitably ominous – it had been closed down. New locks on the doors and signs on the window saying that it had ceased trading. I was told to move the contents of my bedroom from the hotel (during the school holidays I was living 'above the shop') to the semi-detached house next door but one. That meant making the short journey from number 357 London Road to number 361: the single, semi-detached house two doors down from the hotel, which my mother had bought during the good times, aka the Monopoly Years. For me, moving wasn't a big deal, as by this time I'd got used to carting my stuff somewhere else at a moment's notice. In those days I changed

bedrooms more often than most people changed their under-
pants. It was one of the consequences of having a) a home that
doubled as a hotel and b) a mother like mine.

Although the Nonsuch was now empty, it remained within
tantalizingly easy reach: about 20 yards away. I couldn't not go
there, of course. After all, I'd been born in it and spent large
parts of my childhood there. One day, a few months after it had
been closed down, my curiosity inevitably got the better of me.
I remember climbing over the back fences separating 361 from
357 to see what had become of it.

It was weird. On the very large, over-the-top, concrete
Italianate patio with 15-foot-high walls that my mother had
built out the back, much to the annoyance of the neighbours, lay
several small crates of bottled beer, unopened. Looking through
the glass doors at the back of the hotel, I could see that the furniture was still in place in the dining room and that all the
catering paraphernalia – large vats of cooking oil, industrial-
sized saucepans and so on – were still in the kitchen. But as far
as any human content was concerned it was dead. The spirit had
finally left the place. It was a suburban version of Pompeii:
everything had been frozen in time, leaving behind clues that
there had once, in this place, been a successful and thriving civ-
ilization. In Pompeii's case, however, they bequeathed us
buildings of awe-inspiring beauty. The implosion of the Nonsuch
left behind two joined-up semi-detached houses and a crap
patio.

The ending of the Good Times meant there was now the not-
very-small matter of school fees to consider. By now I had left
Colditz-on-the-Hill and been sent to board at Epsom College, a
public school a lot closer to home.

One day my housemaster, Mr Lane, called me into his study.
He was a tall, wiry, athletic bloke with scarily bulging blue eyes

who smoked a pipe, once held the British record for throwing the javelin, and used to take a two-and-a-half-pace run-up (rather unfairly, I always thought) when he caned you. He wore the public-school housemaster's regulation uniform: dark brown tweed jacket with a bit of green patterning going on in there, leather patches under the elbows and Hush Puppies. He also had a strange habit of audibly sucking air in through his teeth, in between sentences. Most of the parents who sent their children to Epsom were doctors, lawyers or traditional upper-middle-class professional British types, so he had never met anyone like my mother before. He used to refer to her as 'a remarkable woman' or 'your extraordinary mother'. He was also, as you may have guessed, the husband of Mrs Lane, the small, voluptuous, fiery-maned lady with bright red lipstick and freckles who hauled me out of the French exam the day my mother launched her gay hotel/cancer bombshell on the local public, and then me.

I always felt sick whenever the message came through that Mr Lane wanted to see me, as I always assumed I'd done something wrong and was about to be flogged. I still get that same feeling even now, thirty years on, when I hear my editor wants a word: even though, as yet, none of the dozen or so that I've worked for has shown the slightest interest in corporal punishment. This time, however, Mr Lane's body language – seated, cross-legged, puffing on the pipe, and what just about passed as a look of concern – suggested that my arse was not going to be the centrepiece of this occasion. He had been speaking to my mother, he said, who was a remarkable woman. She had been very ill and so financially, he said, in between a particularly sharp in-gust of breath, things weren't what they were. My mother, who was an extraordinary woman, had therefore told him that she couldn't afford the fees any more and so she was going to have to take me out of school. But Mr Lane didn't want that to happen as he felt I'd made, and could still make, a great contribution to school life. So he had had a word with the people in charge of the college's scholarship fund and from now on, he said, they were going to pay my fees in full. Looking back, I should have been a lot more appreciative than I was.

Our life then got very different, very quickly. My mother informed me that she now had to go out and do a job just like everybody else, to make ends meet. So she took work selling RAC memberships to car owners at motorway service stations. She had also managed to scrape enough money together to put down a deposit on a semi-detached house with five bedrooms in Egmont Road in Sutton, where she, I and my older brother Peter would now live. This was going to be interesting. Although she was my mother, I'd never actually lived with her – in any meaningful way – before. But now it was to be her, me and my brother, all under one roof, trying to live together like normal people for the first time ever. Somewhere along the line it should have occurred to me that it wasn't going to be easy. But it didn't.

20 June 2005

From: Mmaitland @xxxxxx
To: jmaitland@xxxxx
Sent: June 20 2005
Subject: feud for thought

Are you sure you want to write a book on this particular subject? If
you leave a cesspit alone for long enough, it doesn't smell too bad,
provided you keep your distance. But if you start stirring it . . .

PS: Glad to hear you got married. Congratulations. Why wasn't I
invited?

From: jmaitland@xxxxx
To: Mmaitland @xxxxxx
Sent: June 20 2005
Subject: feud for thought

Who said anything about a cesspit? I'm just curious, that's all. And
the use of words like 'cesspit' makes me even more so. Yes, I am

pretty sure I want to write about this. But I need you to help me. If you can't, or don't want to, that's fine. But I was hoping you might be able to . . .

PS: I would have invited you but I honestly didn't think you'd come.

'Cesspit'? What is he on? Has he inherited our mother's flair for hysterical hyperbole? Or does he know something I don't?

22 June 2005

spent this morning learning how to be a conman and this afternoon seeing my aunt. This morning was interesting. My tutor Jay is not and never has been a conman but he knows a lot about successful high-pressure selling. He is the sort of ultra-confident, well-groomed bloke you see in adverts on American TV who promises that 'You too can be rich, if you follow my simple six-week course, costing just $99.99'. Jay spent most of the eighties driving round Britain in a Ford Sierra with his jacket and several clean shirts on hangers in the back, earning 'between three and five grand a week, every week'.

He was selling double glazing – surprise, surprise – but nowa-days he just sells himself. He got bored of being his company's top salesman five years out of eight – 'And that's not easy, let me tell you' – and so now he teaches other people – debt collectors, door-to-door salesmen, etc. – how to succeed. We want to show our viewers how the more sophisticated rogue traders operate and so the idea is for Jay to teach me the art of the high-pressure sell. We will then film me, secretly, trying to scam a few punters in their own homes. I thought I was going to get a lesson in how to charm the pants off prospective customers but no, that's old hat, Jay told me. Thirty years ago, he said, all travelling salesmen used the 'I'm a really nice person, so like me and buy my £499 carpet-cleaning system now' tactic and it worked a treat. Bung in a nice smile, a few jokes and a couple of compliments and you were home and dry six times out of ten. But then, thanks to programmes like ours, said Jay, the punters became wise to these tricks and a new approach was needed. Now, he says, it's all about taking control and manipulating the customer. And that, surprisingly, means being a bit of a wanker. Don't, for instance, stand there pretending to admire your prospective client's taste in interior design. Instead, tell them they have shit wallpaper. No, really. If they tell you to get out, that's fine – you will have saved yourself a lot of wasted time and effort as they have proved, by responding in that fashion, that they cannot be controlled and therefore they will almost certainly not buy your wares, whatever you say or do. It's all about you manipulating them. If they take your criticism on board, they have shown they are manipulable. You – the salesman – will have established a crucial level of control over them and the situation. Now, said Jay, you have them hooked on your bait and all you have to do is reel them in. Blimey, I said. I'm not sure I like that – manipulating people out of their money. Jay countered that there was nothing wrong with getting people to do something they didn't want to – a lot of us do it every day. Take my job, he said. How many times have I talked someone into doing an interview when they were unwilling, or flat-out didn't want to? He had a point, I conceded. But, I pointed out, there's a difference between getting a reluctant interviewee to go on camera and getting an old lady to spend three grand on having an unnecessary and overpriced alarm system fitted. Anyway – I am due to try out Jay's tactics for real some time in the next few weeks.

After that I drove up to north London. My Auntie Ruthie is a

lot like my mother: short, plumpish and definitely no wallflower.
As with all Jewish women of a certain age, when loved ones
come to call, the fridge door gets opened approximately 4.2 seconds after the front one. The food she had laid out on the table
would have caused a riot at Weight Watchers: deep-fried slices of
an onion-batter-herb thing, a vast, gleaming chocolate cake, a
roast chicken that looked as if it had spent the last twelve
months weight-training down the gym and a small hillock of
potato salad in an ornate glass bowl. I glanced around the room.
As always, the same thought struck me. It could have been dec-
orated by my mother. It had well-off, comfortable, London
Jewish written all over it: lots of beige, Middle Eastern carvings
on the wall, deep, plush sofas and thick, shaggy carpets.

'So, darling, you want to find out more about your parents.
Why is this? Why now?'

'I met this bloke the other day and he said some interesting
stuff went on in the sixties with my mother and father and now
is as good a time as any to get to the bottom of it, I guess.'

'But you know, darling, some times . . . you go digging . . .
and you don't like what you find.'

'Fair enough . . . but I'd rather know than not. I mean, what
do you know?'

'There were . . . issues. Issues with the way they behaved. I
don't want to say more. You need to find these things out first
hand, really. It's not fair for me to tell you them. If you can't,
then I will tell you, I promise. But you know, your mother has
always loved you very much.'

'I know, I'm sure. But I can't quite square that with her send-
ing me away to boarding school when I was three.'

'I know, darling, But she had this thing. She really thought she
was doing the best for you. She really did.'

Here comes another soup ingredient, floating to the top. I was three. I was at High Trees, the boarding school in Dorking. It was the last day of term and I was waiting outside the school's main building to be picked up. At first there were about fifty of us – all small boys – waiting expectantly for the crunch of car tyres on gravel, the flick of the car door opening and the sight of the longed-for parent to sweep us up into their arms. One by one our numbers decreased until finally there was just the one left.

'Don't worry, Maitland,' said a grown-up. 'I'm sure someone will be along in a moment.'

I was too nervous and worried to cry. Instead I felt the tartan trousers I was wearing – I have always remembered those tartan trousers: the feel, the look, the smell of them – grow warm and damp. I told nobody. Someone did arrive eventually: I think it was a member of staff from one of the old people's homes.

My flashback was disturbed by a monstrous oven-bronzed chicken and its mistress's voice. 'Here, my darling . . . have some lovely chicken, why don't you?'

Back to reality. I tried getting Ruthie to give me some clues. Was my mother's behaviour more Robert Maxwell than Richard Branson? Or was it low-level Arthur Daley stuff? She wouldn't be drawn and kept trying to change the subject. I got mildly exasperated. I just wanted to know, I asked her, why my mother changed tack, business-wise. One day she was running Twin Gables, the old people's home. And two more besides. The next, Twin Gables had become the Nonsuch Park Hotel.

'Do you know . . . I am not sure,' said Ruthie. 'I have an idea, but I am not sure.'

'What kind of an idea?'

'Darling, I am sure you can find out. You do this job for a living, don't you? Finding things out?'

'Yes, but what a situation! I am an investigative journalist and my quarry is . . . my mother.'

24 June 2005

have just spent a good part of my journey from Sutton Library back home to Chiswick thinking of that character on *The Fast Show* who used to appear from nowhere looking mad and saying things like 'Today, I shall be mostly . . . wearing a candelabra on my head'. That's because today I have been mostly . . . failing dismally. Unless you count as an achievement the discovery that Sutton Library, and indeed Sutton, are far more grim and soulless and horrible than I ever imagined them to be.

When my mother and I lived there, in the late seventies and eighties, I thought it was a great place. I'm not quite sure why. Maybe it's because Sutton is where I just happened to be when, soon after shedding 3 stone on a diet of cheese and biscuits, I discovered the joy of girls and mates. So enamoured with Sutton were Nick (school classmate/near neighbour/fellow trainee hack on the *Sutton and Cheam Guardian*/fellow founder of our cricket team) and I that we vowed to each other that if either of us had a son, his first name would be Glenn. In Nick's case, after the Spurs midfield genius Glenn Hoddle. In mine, after the lead singer of Squeeze, Glenn Tillbrook. His middle name, though,

would be Sutton. As in Glenn Sutton Maitland. It seemed like a
good idea at the time.

All I can say in our defence is that back in those days Sutton
didn't have the horrible one-way system it's got now, i.e. the type
you find in so many anodyne, suburban shit-holes. Or maybe
I've got a bad case of retrospective rose-tinted vision, and Sutton
always was a bit crap and I was too young and too distracted to
notice. The library, surprise, surprise, was just where I had left it,
all those years ago, when I used to sneak off from work early
from the *Sutton Guardian* to scoff doughnuts and drink tea.
There it was, right in the middle of the one-way system, a vast
collection of concrete rectangles which made Prince Charles's
hated National Theatre look like the Sistine Chapel. In Sutton,
however, it fitted in perfectly. Not much else was the same,
though. The first pub I ever went to, the Whistle Stop opposite
the railway station, had disappeared and had been replaced by
something cheap and nasty looking called the Litten Tree. The
offices of the mighty *Sutton and Cheam Guardian*, meanwhile,
which I passed on my way to the library, had turned into a place
called the Famous Academy. I'd love to be able to report that it
is now a top-level academic institution specializing in media and
international relations but it, also, is a pub.

Yes, we do have records of local newspapers, the woman on
the ground floor told me. Top floor, take the lift if you like. Aha.
The top floor. I studied for my first-year law exams at university
here; 1981, wasn't it? I sat right there, at a desk with a good view
of the rest of the floor, so I could ogle women in between trying
to work out what tort, negligence and promissory estoppel were.
The woman in the archive department was encouraging.

'We go a long way back, dear. We've got all the local papers,
the oldest is from 1881. They're all on microfilm. That drawer
over there.'

Hmm. Where to start? The small box marked 'Sutton and Cheam Advertiser 63–65'? Or 'Epsom and Ewell Herald 66–68'? It's roll-your-sleeves-up time.

Eight and three-quarter hours and one vile portion of lemon meringue pie later (what happened to all those lovely dough-nuts?), my brain was beginning to slip its moorings. It was time to give up. Today, I have been mostly achieving . . . nothing. Apart from working out how something called a Kodak Micro Film Reading Machine works. I never want to see one of these things again but I suspect I'm going to have to. The machine, as the name suggests, is a device for reading vast amounts of old newspaper articles quickly without getting your fingers dirty. Because the articles are on film and not on paper, you obviously don't have the problem that afflicts all old newspapers and people, i.e. the ageing process that makes them grow tatty, yellow, and eventually fall apart. The machine has a big screen, underneath which is a spooling system. Once you've put the right bit of the film in the right place and clicked a couple of levers, hey presto, you are suddenly confronted with the local paper headlines – and the rest – of more than forty years ago. It's quite a novelty and not unenjoyable. At first, anyway. It was like one of those old black-and-white film sequences that signified the passage of a long period of time. But instead of dates on the calendar whizzing past my eyes, I was seeing newspaper head-lines whir by. Non-stop. For hour upon hour.

I did it, though: I spooled through every frame of every reel of microfilm, and inspected every page of every local newspaper from 1963 to 1965, scanning each and every headline for men-tions of my mother my father, or their old people's homes, of which they owned (depending on the year) between two and four. Nothing. But there were some corking headlines. Such as:

'UNINSURED DRIVER HIT FENCE'. Oh, and 'TWO MEN SLEPT IN DERELICT HOUSE AND STOLE LEAD FROM ROOF.' Oh dear. I don't even know what I'm looking for. It may not even exist . . . This is going to take a lot longer than I thought.

25–30 June 2005 and
1964/1966/1975

have just spent the last five evenings on the trot in Sutton Library's newspaper archive department. My wife thinks I'm having an affair. And I am: with the Kodak Micro Film Reading Machine. At times, the prospect of watching porridge grow cold seemed infinitely more pleasurable. Occasionally, however, sandwiched between the long hours of relentless boredom, were small glints of sharp, revealing light. I actually succeeded in finding articles about my mother. And my father. Their businesses, my past. My home. Things I never knew. Things I thought I knew but had recalled inaccurately. Things I have described in this book but remembered imperfectly. Some of the articles were small and, to the rest of the population of the world, laughably prosaic and tedious. But not to me.

The first one I came across was from page 5 of the *Epsom and Ewell Advertiser and Reporter* of Thursday, 23 January 1964. It was nestling between an advert for RACS, the local electrical store, which declared it was 'Ready for BBC2', and a short piece entitled 'THE MITCHAM SOUND', which informed readers:

'Mitcham's answer to the Beatles, Tony Rae and the Emblems, attracted more than 400 teenagers to a dance at the Baths Hall, Mitcham last week, in aid of a proposed youth centre.' The piece that lit up my morning, however, was this:

LUXURY HOME FOR THE ELDERLY

An elderly people's home with all the comforts of a luxury hotel is being built in Epsom and should be open by the end of February.

The home, which is the brainchild of Mr I. B. Maitland who already owns old people's homes in Cheam and Ewell, will cater for men and women over retiring age.

The home will have fitted carpets in all rooms, wash basins in all the single and double bed-sitting rooms, large communal lounge and dining room, special sunken baths, brand new furniture – and no rules or regulations.

Breakfast in Bed

Numerous luxuries will be provided by Mr Maitland – among them early morning tea, breakfast in bed, a choice of menus at every meal, eating either in bed-sitting rooms or in the communal dining room, and a large garden with deck chairs and sun shades.

All this Mr Maitland claims he can supply for £9 9s. a week.

The house, which is in Longdown Road, was described by Mr. Maitland as 'too large for modern families but perfect for my purpose'. It is in grounds of over an acre and at present in the hands of decorators and other tradesmen. The house will have a capacity for 12 people who will be looked after by nursing orderlies. A specialist will visit the house once a week, and National Health doctors will be available.

Phew! The Dead Sea Scrolls it ain't, I grant you. It may have had a narcotic effect on all those who read it at the time (if anyone did) but today, in 2005, it rocked my world. The person who wrote the article all those years ago could never have known how euphoric his little banalities would make someone, thirty-nine years later. I felt a small but substantial sense of triumph once I'd found this piece. There might be a long way to go, but at least I was on the right path. At least there was something there. It was as if I'd reached base camp at the foot of Mount Everest. And I had reassessed those two years I spent as a trainee on the borough's favourite birdcage floor-liner, otherwise known as the *Sutton and Cheam Guardian.* Some of the pieces I wrote back then were so parochial, mind-numbing and trite, I couldn't believe they mattered to anyone. But now I know different – someone, somewhere, one day, might be hanging on to my every typed word from 1983.

After that I came across an average of one piece a day. Hard going: but to paraphrase Magnus Magnusson when he used to present *Mastermind*, now I've started, it seems silly not to try and finish. One afternoon I thought, for a moment, that I'd found something potentially very interesting. That was when the following headline blared out at me from page 3 of the *Sutton and Cheam Herald* of Friday, 28 January 1966: 'MOTHER REMOVED AFTER HOUR AT OLD PEOPLE'S HOME'.

But it didn't amount to very much at all.

> Retired schoolmaster Mr John H. H. Sharpe took his 99 year old mother into Rose Gates, a home for the elderly at Sutton, but was dissatisfied with the welcome she received and removed her after an hour. He also stopped the cheque he had given.
>
> At Epsom County Court last week the proprietor, Mr Irving

B. Maitland of Grove Road, Sutton, sued Mr Sharpe for £38 4s
6d damages for alleged breach of contract . . .

And so it went on. No scandal. And of no interest whatsoever,
except to the people concerned, one of whom – the 99-year-old
mother – had died of natural causes by the time the story had
been written. It was a non-story. Mr Sharpe wasn't happy that
my parents were absent when he brought his mother in. So he
took her out again an hour later. My father said they weren't in
because a resident at another of their homes had had a heart
attack and they had gone to look after her. The judge said fair
enough and so Mr Sharpe had to pay up. End of non-story. I'm
beginning to think that the hack with the roast beef complexion
must have been suffering from a bad case of Chinese whispers.
Maybe this was what Dennis was thinking about when he mentioned embezzlement, only he'd got the wrong end of the stick.

Near the end of the week came the gems. Nothing I didn't
know about, mind you. It was the *Epsom and Ewell Herald* of
3 July 1975. There, on the front page, was the piece that Simon
Rhodes passed to me just before our end-of-year French exam. It
was intcresting to compare the reality of what was in front of me
with the account I had written for this book. My memory had
been serving me relatively well but there was a lot of detail I had
forgotten. It was a chance to press the action replay button in
my memory, to live it all again: this time through the eyes and
words of journalists, neighbours and key players. The front page
sported a huge, banner headline: 'EWELL GUEST HOUSE PLANS TO GO
GAY'.

There was much (unintentionally comic) enjoyment to be had
from reading the articles that I couldn't have appreciated at the
time. There were a lot of them, too. They filled the front page
and all of page 2. This was a big one for the *Herald*. I should put

things in context: all this went on in the deeply conservative (and Conservative) borough of Epsom and Ewell, where painting your half of the drainpipe in any colour other than black marked you down as a possible danger to society. My mother had already outraged the locals by opening a hotel in the first place. When it was used as an old people's home it was fine – not too many late night discos or drunken behaviour to worry about – but a guest house was a different proposition entirely. She hit the ground running from the off. She announced the arrival of the Nonsuch Park Hotel by decking out the front with a hideously garish bright orange canopy, four enormous flagpoles and a vast red-and-white sign which, helpfully, became brightly lit at night. This wouldn't have mattered much if the hotel had been located in, say, downtown Los Angeles. But the Nonsuch was the result of two 1930s semi-detached houses that had been knocked together and was right in the middle of a 3-mile stretch of identical-looking dwellings which, despite their hideous soullessness, housed some proud and not very broad-minded owners. Decking the place out apparently in readiness for a poofs' tea party – which is what it was now becoming – was never going to make her the most popular person in town. Now she was about to be positively reviled.

It was fascinating, all these years later, to see it splashed across the paper like this. I had spent so many years telling people about it that it had become more story than reality. But here it was. It really did happen. In the middle of the front page there was a photo of my mother with the hotel behind her. She was holding her arms aloft, like Moses. Just above her head was a sign saying 'Nonsuch Park Hotel'. The 'o' in 'hotel', however, had slipped and was hanging forlornly at right angles. Unlike my mother, who was smiling and, according to the caption, was the 'Defiant, vivacious owner of the Nonsuch Hotel, Mrs Bru

Wynton: "I've no time to worry about what the neighbours think. I'm doing what I want and keeping to the rules".'

The front-page article, meanwhile, thundered:

> Shock plans to turn a hotel into a 'gay guest house' for homosexual couples this week raised a storm of protest in Ewell.
>
> Figure behind the scheme, Nonsuch Park Hotel owner Mrs Bru Wynton, said: 'I want to pep up the area – put some life into the rows of houses which are all the same.'
>
> But residents near the eight year old hotel – in London Road opposite Nonsuch Park – have pledged themselves to fight the proposals at all costs.
>
> 'There will be one hell of a protest. We have become used to the unexpected from Mrs Wynton but this is a bombshell,' said Mr David Wiltshire, a next door neighbour.
>
> The feud between Mrs Wynton and her neighbours – which has been going on since the two semi detached houses were developed into a guest house – reached new heights of bitterness when it was revealed that Nonsuch Hotel would no longer be catering just for business executives.
>
> It was going all out to attract a gay clientele.
>
> Mrs Wynton has already employed a full time manager, 28 year old Carl, whose previous experience includes running a 623 roomed gay hotel in Amsterdam.
>
> 'This will be a great challenge. In Amsterdam, homosexuality is accepted.
>
> 'But here in Ewell I will have to fight the traditional English reserve which makes them backwards in treating us equally,' he said on Friday.
>
> 'People tend to think: "Oh, we don't have people like that living round here" – well I know 60 gay people in Ewell, never mind Epsom or Sutton,' he added.

He predicted that guests would have started arriving today (Thursday) but his long term aim is to attract trade from abroad, as well as locally.

'I am determined to get together an efficient staff of six ready to cope with the influx we are expecting, once our existence gets around.

'I have never known a gay guest house to run at a loss.'

Not only has Mrs Wynton's plan meant a change of clientele but also a change of name. Her two favourites are 'The Gay Guest House' or 'Homolulu'.

She is going ahead with the backing of her lawyers and has booked an advertisement in *Gay News*, a newspaper with a circulation of 20,000.

A *Gay News* spokesman described her plan as 'terrific'.

'This could be the most advanced hotel idea in the world. For Mrs Wynton is discriminating against no one.

'The idea of straight and gay people mixing in the same place may be too idealistic – but if it catches on, terrific,' he said.

He said it was the first time gay people had managed to establish a centre in the Epsom area.

'This is a very residential area. The nearest other places are clubs in Wimbledon or Guildford.

'Otherwise to meet gay people would mean a trip to London,' he said.

Claims that the plan was being done 'out of spite' were strongly denied by Mrs Wynton.

'I've had enough trouble with neighbours or officials in the past. Well now, I'm keeping to the rules.

'It will be run according to the official regulations – only for the guests.

'They will be charged the same as straight people: £6 for a double room, £4 single,' she said.

But residents and some of the clergy are 'appalled'.

Neighbour Mr Roger Barnard fears for the safety of his two young children – 'And I'm sure every parent will regard this as an abomination.'

Stoneleigh Baptist Pastor, the Rev Peter Nash said: 'I'm appalled. She may not be breaking the law, but the moral point of view is something different.

'These people need help, not encouragement to pursue their perversions.'

Neighbour Mr Ronald Neills summed up their feelings: 'I run Victoria Station during the day and you get all sorts there. I've no intention of coming home at night and finding myself living next door to a poofter house.'

Borough Development Officer Mr Kenneth Spelman said: 'we are watching this very carefully and will compare the facts with the statements we find in our town planning encyclopaedia – it's our bible.

'As a local authority we have to be very open minded.'

'My hotel for homosexuals' – see page two

And there, on page 2, were five follow-up stories. Some repeated what had been said on the front but there were still more extracts from the World According to Bru Wynton. There was also an editorial at the top of the page, written by '*Herald* Chief Reporter Donna Leigh':

GOING 'GAY' – AND SPLITTING THE COMMUNITY

A guest house for homosexuals – 'lesbians welcome' – in the middle of what must be one of the most typically middle class, suburban areas in Britain. That is the plan.

And had Epsom's gypsies been allocated Nonsuch Park as

their permanent campsite, the shock could hardly have been greater for local residents.

The idea is the brainchild of Mrs Bru Wynton, vivacious owner of the Nonsuch Park Hotel guest house on the London Road, Ewell.

She wants to completely change the image of this hotel – which caters for commercial travellers and in its eight year existence has already achieved local notoriety – in order to 'pep up' the area.

The official opening date is fixed for the end of July and an advertisement has been booked in the international newspaper *Gay News*, which has a circulation of 20,000.

But, said new manager, 28 year old Carl, 'The build up has already started. News of this guest house is being spread by our amazingly effective grape vine. And by the time the *Herald* appears on Thursday, our guests will have started arriving.'

So, all of a sudden, local residents have found themselves face to face with the implications of the permissive society and its Anti-Discrimination Bill. Not at the switch of a TV dial, but disconcertingly in the flesh.

They are learning that today's meaning of 'queen', 'queer' and 'gay' – synonymous with homosexual – are startlingly different from the dictionary definitions they were given at school.

Mrs Wynton's actions pose the dilemma: 'What moral standpoint should I take?' And they threaten to split a community right down the middle because, as our *Herald* inquiries reveal, no one feels they can afford to remain indifferent to this issue.

What follows are exclusive interviews with gay manager Carl, the hotel's nearest neighbours, local clergymen, members of Stoneleigh Residents Association – and the controversial figure behind the scheme, Mrs Wynton, explaining her motives and opinions.

By the way: you might just be asking yourself – a lot of people have, over the years – about the origins of the name 'Nonsuch'. Well, legend has it that King Henry V111 – a man who, like my mother, was no stranger to the divorce courts – used to like staying in the splendid mansion house in the park's grounds. One fine day he is supposed to have looked out of his window – while demolishing a large chicken leg and deciding who to marry next, no doubt – at the marvellous view, and declared: 'There is non such park as this!' And that was that.

Some 400 years later, local residents were now finding that there was also non such hotel as this, nor non such owner. The biggest story on page 2 carried the headline: '"MY HOTEL FOR HOMOSEXUALS" – WOMAN EXPLAINS'.

Mrs Bru Wynton has been married twice but is now independent – 'The way I like it' – and has four children by her first marriage.

The eldest is 28 year old daughter Rachel, who lives in Stoneleigh and her three sons are 25, 21 and 14.

Nonsuch Hotel owner for eight years, Mrs Wynton said the idea of the gay guest house would be to have 'straight' and 'gay' visitors mixing in the way her children communicate with them.

'Most people talk as if gay people are a different species, freaks even. Too often they believe gays are out to corrupt children.

'Well, I have worked with these people for a long time in the catering business and would not fear for my sons' spiritual welfare if they were left with them.'

Daughter Rachel interrupted: 'I thought my mother's idea was odd at first but then she always has unusual suggestions which eventually turn out to everyone's advantage.

'As for gay people corrupting morals, it's rubbish. In my experience they look after my two youngsters better than a woman I hired to do the job.'

Mrs Wynton strongly believes homosexuality is environmental: 'treating gays like outcasts only aggravates their problem.

'By pushing homosexuality into the back streets and separating them from the rest of society what hope in heaven have you got of helping them?

'I don't believe their behaviour is of genetic origin – I feel it's environmental and given the chance, they would be able to form normal relationships,' she said.

Mrs Wynton admitted the history of her guest house has not been a smooth one.

Last year there was a public inquiry which alleged breaches of planning control. As a result she was allowed to keep certain buildings developed without planning permission – but others had to go.

The final blow was dealt last week when she failed to persuade the Borough's Environment and Health Committee to grant her a singing and dancing licence.

'I thought of selling out and even put the house on the market but I have decided not to throw in the towel.

'I'm fed up with my neighbours' objections. Everything I have wanted to do – even trivialities like flying flags – has been turned down.

'Well, now they should be satisfied. I will keep to the rules – the guest house will be run only for the guests.

'Music will be provided only by a disco as no planning permission is necessary.'

Mrs Wynton has spoken to lawyers and gay advisors and said there is nothing anyone can do to stop her.

'I love living and I want to do as much living my way as I can,' she said.

Mrs Wynton is suffering from incurable cancer and has been told she has only a year or two left.

'It could come in the form of a heart attack or cancer so I gain nothing by being mercenary. I haven't got time to waste squabbling with neighbours.'

The hotel has been running on a skeleton staff of three since its owner was forced to go to hospital.

And it was during this continuous period of drug taking and operations that she first thought of setting up a gay guest house.

'The people who helped me through this painful time did not include my "straight" husband but my children and former gay manager, Edward.

'Such tenderness and care he showed me, I was able to get over the psychological depression.'

From a business point of view, Mrs Wynton says the Nonsuch area is an ideal spot for a gay hotel.

It's residential, opposite a historical park and within easy travelling distance of Epsom Downs, Hampton Court and London.

'This area is discreet so I am still trying to decide whether the name "Homolulu" is too flamboyant. To survive in this business one must be a bit of a showman – but I do understand there are those who would feel embarrassed at being so obviously identified – and the title would put them off from staying here.

'I see no need to inform prospective "straight" guests of the conversion. If they object they will have their money refunded. I do not want to be surrounded by such narrow minded types in my place.'

Mrs Wynton predicts a drop in the market value of her

property and that of the surrounding area. 'If that happens then I will be delighted to buy out my next door neighbours.'

Mrs Wynton is in the peculiar position of owning two semi detached houses either side of her immediate neighbours, who refuse to sell to her.

The story underneath, which carried the headline '"MANY GAY LOCALS" – MANAGER', featured more comments from the 'tall, blond and well-groomed 28 year old Carl', whose existence I had never known about until now and who, the paper said, was 'a former naval lieutenant who has been in the hotel trade for five and half years'. The gist, again, was that there were an awful lot more gay people living in the area than you might think, and he knew what he was talking about, nudge nudge wink wink. The piece also said that Carl had 'several "contracts" in the Surrey area'. I think they meant to say 'contacts'. Maybe they were having trouble with their 'r's.

Then there was a story with the headline '"BROADMINDED" – "APPALLED"', which featured two local ministers, both pictured, one of whom was the Reverend Peter Nash, who was clearly working himself into quite a lather about the prospect of widespread homosexuality in his parish. Here on page 2 he developed his theory, first seen on page 1, that the whole thing was immoral, deplorable and perverted. 'I never imagined this would happen in Stoneleigh,' he was quoted as saying. 'This is an area of married couples with young children. How are they going to feel with gay people living among them?' The Reverend Finnan, on the other hand, took a different view. 'I am broadminded on this . . . if I met a "gay" person walking down the street, my attitude to them wouldn't be any different than to anybody else I would meet.'

There was also more stuff from the neighbours. Some of it was very entertaining. Under the heading 'ONE HELL OF A PROTEST

CERTAIN – NEIGHBOUR', a bloke called Roger Barnard, who lived in a house that 'backs onto the controversial property', said: 'It saddens me that Mrs Wynton should degrade herself and others in this way. I hope the authorities will do something about it.' Mr Barnard's neighbour, Mr Wiltshire, was more restrained: 'I take a cynically resigned line. We have come to expect a lot of things from Mrs Wynton but it does seem a surprising development for a house which is supposed to cater for business executives.' But Mr Ronald Neills, who lived right next door, was the most forthright of all. Referring to the guests at what he called 'The Poofter House', he said: 'If I come across any of them, there's going to be trouble alright.'

My mother's PR machine must have been working well because in the same paper, just a week later, there was a story on the front page entitled: 'GAY HOTEL IS A HIT'.

> The gay hotel for homosexuals in North Cheam is already a great success, according to its owner.
>
> Mrs Bru Wynton, owner of the Nonsuch Park Hotel in London Road, said yesterday: 'It is already a wild success and we are not even open officially in our new style until the end of this month.'
>
> Mrs Wynton, who for two years has run a hotel near Chichester on similar lines, added, 'The Nonsuch Park Hotel has at last got sparkle.
>
> 'There have been some offensive phone calls, but I don't know what all the fuss is about.'

Then, finally, two weeks later, the inevitable follow up:

POISON CALLS FOR 'GO-GAY' HOTEL

Poison pen letters and a series of obscene telephone calls have followed the shock change over of the Nonsuch Park Hotel into a 'gay guest house' for homosexual couples.

But the newly employed staff of four led by Dutch manager Carl told the *Herald* this week: 'We have been disgusted by what people have only dared say anonymously over the phone but if they think they can prevent us from making this business a success they are wrong. We are determined to treat their comments with the contempt they deserve.'

They have received more than twenty calls denouncing the proposal of a gay clientele as 'sordid, filthy, disgusting and revolting.'

An anonymous letter addressed to Mrs Bru Wynton, owner of 'The Poofter's Paradise Hotel', has been described by Carl as a typical reaction of those bitterly opposed to the plan.

The writer says: 'The unfortunate human beings who indulge in this utterly revolting and unnatural act termed homosexuality are bound to be pitied. That you should endeavour to cash in on their misfortunes is, to say the least, a despicable business.'

The letter ends with a vow to give Nonsuch Hotel staff 'hell in every possible direction until everyone involved in the venture flushes down the drain.'

Mrs Bru Wynton retorted: 'It's nothing more than can be expected from a narrow minded and ignorant attitude. I personally invite neighbours and objectors to come inside and meet my staff.'

There has been one letter of support from The Rev Mark Hill of St Nicholas' Church, Sutton. 'I cannot find anything unnatural or morally wrong with this expression of sexuality for those Christians who do indulge in this kind of thing. It's too often largely based upon a lack of information and a wrong understanding of Holy scripture,' he said.

'Is it not time that our so called 'free and just society'

extended some of those qualities to this sizeable minority and ceased this ill informed persecution? It's my hope that Mrs Wynton's hotel may contribute something to the education of our community.'

There have been three cancellations since the 'go-gay' plans were announced, but after the initial shock all the 'straight' guests, including an American businessman, his wife and two children, have said they are quite satisfied with the change of management.

The nearest to any physical trouble started when a group of youths started shouting outside the hotel. 'But when two of my staff went outside to talk to the lads, they just ran off,' said Carl.

'Our only other regret is the attitude of the neighbours. We have had complaints about the discos we held on Thursday, Friday and Sunday evenings. But when the police investigated, we explained that we held a phonographic and restaurant licence and they were satisfied,' said Carl.

Residents are to meet tomorrow (Friday) to discuss what action, if any, they should take. Stoneleigh Ward Councillor Mr Leonard Miller said: 'My personal opinion is that this plan is outrageous. Obviously it will be debated on Friday and I can see a petition eventually being drawn up.'

And that, for the time being, was where the local newspaper coverage of my mother ceased. No explanation of why the old people's homes had suddenly turned into hotels. Plenty of scandal, sure: but nothing I didn't know about. Not exactly dodgy, either. In fact rather open-minded and courageous. And ahead of her time: the Pink Pound hadn't even been invented then. It didn't work out, of course, and the hotel was closed within eighteen months. But she had her fun. And she clearly loved baiting the neighbours and the council. Depending on your point of view, that's either highly praiseworthy or totally irresponsible. I veer towards the former but I am biased. It's funny, but I never even talked about all those front (and second) page stories about cancer, homosexuality and death with my mother. She never attempted to give me any explanation, either. She must have had a reason, I think, for choosing to share the details of her illness and her interesting new plans for our home with the citizens of Epsom and Ewell before divulging them to her youngest son. Then again maybe her hunger for publicity simply obliterated all sense of parental duty. Or maybe she just forgot to tell me the stories were being printed. Or maybe she thought I'd never see them anyway.

It made for an unusual home life, that's for sure. Especially when I tried to get my head round some of the sights that now greeted me when I left the 'private' bit of the hotel and ventured down into the area reserved for our gay guests. One night, aged fourteen, pyjama-clad and en route to the hotel kitchens, I remember being transfixed by the sight of two men in see-through flowery shirts and extremely tight black trousers passionately kissing each other in the hotel bar. They were also, I couldn't help noticing, vigorously rubbing their pelvises against each other. All this . . . when the only thing I wanted was a cup of cocoa.

The neighbours' retaliation, predictably enough, soon manifested itself in the form of a series of complaints to the local council. Surely, they argued, she didn't have permission to put up that huge red-and-white sign. Or those flagpoles. Or those big wooden sheds out the back. And they were right. She didn't. But the neighbours were to end up even more frustrated when, for reasons that were (understandably) never explained to them, the council found in her favour. This unexpected ruling may have had something to do with the conversation she had with a high-

ranking officer from the council's planning department who had
come on an official visit to see whether planning laws were being
flouted. It went something like this:

COUNCIL OFFICER (typical of the species: white, middle-aged,
unremarkable): 'So, Mrs Maitland. These sheds. They
are permanent structures. I don't believe we have any
record of you having applied for planning permission for
them.'

MRS MAITLAND: 'Planning permissions? What is planning
permissions? What harm is garden sheds? Look. I give
you this. [Stuffs £100 in cash into officer's hand.] Now
you agree with me?'

COUNCIL OFFICER: 'Mrs Maitland, I couldn't possibly . . .'

MRS MAITLAND: 'Don't be stupid. [Stuffs another £100 or so
into officer's remaining hand.] Why you not buy your
wife nice dinner?'

COUNCIL OFFICER: 'Well, Mrs Maitland, that's really very
kind of you . . .'

Back to the present day, though. I'm beginning to think the
beef-faced hack got his wires crossed: that the perceived skeleton
in the family closet was in fact nothing of the sort. Maybe he
was remembering all this gay hotel business and thought that
qualified for skeleton status. I know Dennis talked about some
kind of embezzlement, but one man's embezzlement is another
man's shrewd business deal. If there had been something really
dodgy going on – like, really dodgy – he surely would have
known about it. And being an ex-copper, he would have done
something about it, too. I have no doubt my mother sailed very
close to the wind but I'm as sure as I can be that she didn't fall
into the water. That leaves my Auntie Ruthie, who told me that

if I went digging, I might not like what I found . . . well, that's hardly sufficient evidence to convict, is it? Maybe Ruthie was guilty of a mild bit of mischief-making. It does run in the family, after all. Or maybe she was viewing my mother's unusual – and sometimes mildly questionable – behaviour through a distorting prism of disapproval. It can happen, and often has.

Do you know something? I'm not sure there's any more digging to do.

2 July 2005

may have been wrong about that.

From: mmaitland @xxxxxxxxx
To: Jmaitland@xxxxxx
Sent: July 2 2005 18.18
Subject: book

OK, I'll help you. I don't know how far you've got but there are some things you might be interested in. There is one incident in particular that has always stuck in my mind. Frustratingly however, I can't remember one or two key details.

I remember seeing a letter, in the early 70s, in a file in the Nonsuch Park Hotel. It was from our mother's solicitor, Benson and Co. It was about a man called Stern and his will. Stern as in Stern and Parsons, the famous estate agents. He was a resident at the Twin Gables old people's home and very rich. There was a lot of money in the family. I remember seeing words like 'problems' and 'trouble' in the letter, but I can't recall exactly what it was about. You could always try digging up the will, if you've got the time and inclination. With luck it should be stored at Probate House in High Holborn. But it will be quite a job. You will have to go through all the wills of everyone called Stern who died between 1963 and 1970. But if you find it, it could give you some very useful clues. Even better, talk to Humphrey Benson himself – if he's still alive. I feel there might well be something worth investigating.

Also, our mother wrote a book called 'The Death Sentence' in the late seventies. It was an autobiography and I have the only copy. It is in a file in the lock up shed at my flat in Hammersmith. If you call there, speak to my tenant and tell him what it's about. I have already told him to expect your call. He will give you instructions on how to get into the shed. The file is in the top shelf on the left as you walk in.

Maurice

Hmm. If there one's thing guaranteed to get a reporter's investigative juices flowing, it's when the words 'trouble' and 'will' are used in the same sentence. When I did my law degree there were no end of cases in which the latter involved a bit of the former. And in some of those cases, what went on ranged from the unsavoury to the downright criminal. Game on again.

7 July 2005

On what was not a great day in the history of investigative journalism I drove down to Epsom with two aims
and failed pathetically to achieve either. My first goal
was to track down the flamboyant and very tall Humphrey
Benson, my mother's solicitor in the sixties and seventies. God,
he must have done well out of her. When she walked though the
door he must have felt like the chairman of a non-league football
team who's just spotted Roman Abramovich in the stands.
Humphrey, I vaguely recollect, always seemed to be at my
mother's beck and call. But who could blame him? She could
turn a law firm's balance sheet from red to black in the space of
one afternoon. As Dennis told me in Malaga, if the tradesmen of
North Cheam, Ewell and Epsom had a Most Popular Punter of
the Year award, she would have won it, hands down, for a
decade. This was a woman with money to spend – and she liked
spending it. As Dennis put it: 'They all thought she was a bit
mad, all right, but if she wanted the last brick on the chimney,
she could 'ave it.' But anyway. Back to Humphrey. He, I reckoned, must know more than anyone what really went on back
then. There was one problem, I thought, as I headed past Epsom

Baths and into the High Street. What if the flamboyant and very tall Humphrey Benson was now also very dead? He must have been in his forties when he was dealing with my mother, which would make him well into his seventies now. If he'd actually made it into his seventies at all, that is.

I also wanted to check out the Nonsuch Park Hotel, previously Twin Gables, as I hadn't set foot in there for more than thirty years. Now seemed like a good time to put that right. And the new owner, I figured, might yield a few juicy titbits about the events of the 1960s and early seventies. He might even know something I didn't. So I parked up just outside Lester Bowden, the legendary men's outfitters in Epsom High Street (est. 1807), which, I noticed, had exactly the same shop sign and window display as it did when my mother used to send me there before the start of term to be kitted out in regulation short trousers and the rest, more than a quarter of a century ago.

That familiarity felt unexpectedly comforting. What followed didn't. 'Hello, Nonsuch Park Hotel?' The voice was flat, male and not very welcoming.

'Ah, yes. Can I speak to the manager, the owner, even, if he's there. Or she.'

'Speaking.'

'Ah, right. I was hoping you could help me, because my mother used to own the Nonsuch, many years ago, and I'm writing a book about it and I thought it might be a good idea to just come and have a chat with you about it, if you were up for it, and also maybe have a look round to see what the place is like now, because I was actually born there, you know, in the hotel, in one of the rooms, although it wasn't a hotel at the time, it was an old people's home. So, er, I wondered if I could maybe pop by.'

'What was your mother's name?'

'Mrs Wynton, you might know her as. Or Mrs Maitland. But

she was Mrs Melman for a time. I think there may have been a Mrs Newman at some stage as well, actually. But, yes, Mrs Wynton. That was the main one.'

Silence.

I'm not good at silence. Oh dear, I thought, I should have gone for Plan B and pretended to be a guest. Turn up, tune in and snoop out. I realized I had been waiting for all of three and three-quarter seconds for a reply that didn't appear to be forthcoming so I jumped in again.

'So . . . how about it?'

'What? How about what?'

'Me sort of . . . coming round. For a nice chat, that's all. Could be quite interesting.'

'We're very busy at the moment. But if you're in the area, try calling.'

'Funnily enough I am, actually. I'm just outside Lester Bowden. Five minutes away. I could pop round now.'

'Like I said, we're very busy.'

'Oh, I just remembered, I'm in Epsom tomorrow, actually, as it happens. Playing cricket at the college. How does that fit in?'

'We're busy throughout the weekend. It's a very busy time.'

'Oh, OK, another time, then. Who should I ask for, by the way?'

'Myself, Graham, or my wife, Linda.'

'OK, I'll do that. Thanks.'

My still, small inner voice of calm – the one that was telling me my phone etiquette needed working on – was about to become a raging inner roar.

'Hello, Benson and Co.?' This time it was an abrupt-sounding schoolmistress type.

'Aha! Hello. I'm trying to track down Humphrey Benson, actually. Is he still there by any chance?'

'Who's speaking, please?'

'My name is Jonathan Maitland and my mother was a good friend of his and I'm trying to track him down because I want him to help me, because I'm a journalist and I'm writing a book, you see.'

'Mr Benson doesn't work here any more.'

'Well, can I speak to someone who does? Like your boss, for example?'

'About what exactly?'

'I . . . I'll tell them when I tell them. Is he around, by the way, Mr Benson, do you know?'

'No, I don't.'

'Well, can you at least pass a message on to your boss and get him to ring me?'

'If you leave your details I'll see what I can do.'

I wanted to chew my knuckles off. Why won't these people help me? Why are they so suspicious? Is it me? Maybe it's the J word: some people would sooner come into contact with fungal nail infection than a journalist.

There was one more avenue, though. And it was just round the corner. When I was an unfeasibly fat and friendless (or so I thought) 13-year-old, the only person who would ever have anything to do with me during the school holidays was a bloke in my class called Hamish. His father owned an estate agency business right in the middle of Epsom High Street, yards away from good old Lester Bowden's, where I was now, fiddling with my mobile. In the summer of 1974 Hamish used to cycle round to the Nonsuch every so often to say hello. I was really grateful: I couldn't believe he wanted anything to do with me, let alone be my friend. I really looked up to him. He was tall, good-looking, in the 'A' team at rugby, and knew girls. He was everything I wasn't and he did everything I didn't. He also, because he had come round unexpectedly one day, knew my deep, dark secret: that I used to wear my school uniform in the holidays. Because I was so fat. Because they were the only clothes that would fit me. And now, more than thirty years on, he was still a friend. And running his dad's business. And one of his colleagues dealt with Benson and Co. a lot. And she knew the bloke who'd run the firm since the seventies, who'd just retired. His name was Nick Carstairs; he was a very nice man indeed and he liked restoring old sports cars. What was more, he lived in Epsom. Just round the corner from Benson and Co. If anyone knew where Humphrey was or wasn't, nice Mr Carstairs did.

Hardly a breakthrough, I know. More of an indentation. And let's not forget it's my own mother I am investigating, not an anonymous, elusive criminal from Romford. So I should be making more progress than I am. But maybe there is nothing to find out. Then again, reading between the lines of Maurice's e-mail, there seems to be. He appears to know more than he is prepared to say. I'm not sure why, though. And what about my Aunt Ruthie? She told me that I might not like what I find. Why would she have said that? If I was doing this story for TV, what's more, there would be One Big Unanswered Question keeping me in the hunt. Why were my mother's old people's homes closed down? She wouldn't have done it voluntarily as they were always full and, I assume, doing a roaring trade. I should find out why. Actually, it's more than that. I *need* to find out why.

Back to the job in hand, though. I established that nice Mr Carstairs, Humphrey Benson's erstwhile colleague from years ago, was ex-directory. So I went round there. But he wasn't in. Out restoring sports cars, no doubt. It was time to employ the written word in the hope it would serve me better than the spoken one.

Dear Mr Carstairs

Sorry to bother you, but I am writing a book about my mother, who was a client – and a good friend – of Humphrey Benson's. I am trying to track Humphrey down, but so far have had very little success. I was wondering if you might be able to help me. I would be very grateful if you would give me a call, either way.

Yours etc.

Jonathan Maitland

1923–1947

This much I know: my mother was born in 1923, in what is now Israel, but was then Palestine. She was the eldest of seven – six girls and a boy – born to Joseph and Esther Nachmani. They all lived in a modern (for the time) three-storey house perched high on Mount Carmel, which was blessed with stunning views of Haifa. All six daughters were dark, exotic and beautiful. Old Man Nachmani didn't like the idea of his daughters putting it about, so he was pretty strict with them. When my mother – her name is Berouia by the way, but everyone has always called her 'Bru' for short – was eighteen, there was a bit of an Incident. Although I have heard the story of the Incident many times over the years, I have never really thought about it much. Until now, that is.

Old Man Nachmani wasn't the sort of bloke to leave anything to chance, let alone the thing called love. He was a difficult, controlling bully. He had it all planned. There was no way his daughters were going to be left to find suitable men on their own. He was going to do the finding for them, once they had reached the right age. And eighteen was, as far as he was concerned, the right age. So, when Bru hit the milestone, her father found her a suitor. He was called Joseph and he was the hairiest man in town. Apparently he looked as if he was hiding a lady's wig under his shirt.

My mother, on the other hand, had hair issues of her own. She was going though a Bette Davis phase and had arranged her hair in a crown of ringlets on her head, just like Bette had done in her latest film. Trouble was, Bru was just as strong-willed as Bette, or the characters she used to play, and decided that Joseph the Hairy One wasn't to her liking. She, however, was very much to Joseph the Hairy One's liking, and he wasn't giving up.

After several months of heavy-duty wooing my mother finally gave in. But it wasn't quite a done deal. Apparently if you were a young woman in those days, there was a kind of dowry system in place. If you wanted to get married, your father was expected to give you a sum of money to help you along the way. One night, at dinner, Old Man Nachmani told my mother how big her dowry was to be, in front of the rest of the family. She wasn't impressed and asked for more. No way, Old Man Nachmani told her, that's what you're getting.

'If you don't give me any more, I'm going to throw myself out of the window.'

Old Man Nachmani laughed.

'No, I mean it.'

He laughed again.

Up she got. Knives and forks were put down and eight pairs of eyes followed her as she made her way to the window. And out of it.

They heard her as she landed: a soft thud but with hard edges, like the boot closing on a car. She had fallen three storeys.

Old Man Nachmani rushed out and found her lying broken on the ground outside. He lifted her up in his arms and an ambulance was called. She had broken her neck and several ribs. She spent the next six months in hospital.

Logic has never been one of mother's strong points: it's all very well brandishing the ultimate trump card in an argument – i.e. 'If you don't agree with me I'm going to kill myself' – but what happens if you carry out your side of the bargain success-fully? You're not exactly going to be in a position to enjoy the fruits of your win, are you? I have no idea what lies behind this mad, cavalier courage of my mother's: all I know is that her rela-tionship with death – the threat of it, the concept of it, the fact of it – has always been unusually reckless and confrontational.

Anyway: Joseph the Hairy One wasn't heard of again. I think he did a runner once he realized what he was letting himself in for.

8 July 2005

Progress. Of sorts. I woke up this morning to find that a message had been left on my mobile, overnight, by the rather posh-sounding Nick Carstairs. He left his number and asked me to call him back, so I did.

'Hello?'

'Hello, Mr Carstairs? Is that Mr Carstairs?'

'Yes.'

He sounded like a man you could do business with. Chipper and cheery, unlike the two brick walls I'd run into yesterday.

'Yes, look, I'm sorry to, kind of, invade your privacy, like I did by putting that letter through your door.'

'Don't worry, but I think you're going to be disappointed anyway. Before we start, can I just ask the full name of your mother?'

'Berouia, um . . .'

He cut in before I could choose one of the many surnames on offer. 'That's enough. And your father?'

'Irving.'

'Oh, yes. Irving Bernard, wasn't it? Yes, because believe it or not, there were a number of Maitlands that we used to do business with. Right, I remember your mother now, yes. How can I help?'

'Well, first of all, I was just wondering what happened to Humphrey.'

'Ah. Humphrey Benson left the firm in 1972. And that is your first problem. Because that was thirty-three years ago. Erm, now your mother, the Maitlands, stopped instructing us, as far as I can remember, and I can't remember very much – in fact at sixty-nine years of age I can hardly remember what I had for breakfast, ha ha ha, so frankly, Humphrey left, and he went to set up on his own, in Ipswich, which was his home town.'

'Blimey.'

'Yes, that was after he married for the fourth time, and the fourth wife, she, you know, wanted him out of it – they do, these wives. And so he went off to Ipswich, and do you know, quite a lot of clients followed him. And he came back, locally, quite a lot, on visits and things, and I've got a funny feeling your mother may possibly have carried on being his client when he went there. I don't think we continued to act for her . . .'

'I remember him being . . . he was kind of . . . tall and flamboyant, wasn't he?'

'Very, very much so. Yes, he was. After all, I mean his grandfather was an Admiral of the Fleet, and the family did all sorts of things. I mean the mother was the first lady barrister in Gray's Inn, in the country. I mean, why he ended up in a potty little dump like Epsom I don't know, ha ha ha.'

'Is he still around, do you know?'

'He's gone abroad.'

'He's still alive!'

'He's still alive, oh yes.'

'You're kidding!'

'On no, he's about seventy-three, seventy-four.'

'Thank God. I thought he might have had it!'

'No, no, no, about seventy-three, seventy-four.'

'Oh my God, well, that's great, because that means I can contact him, because my next question is, um, well . . . it's . . . he . . . you see . . . this book . . . my mother, I am just trying to work out what, if anything, went on in the sixties . . .'

'Well, I'm not going to say anything.' He laughed. Having listened back to it, on tape, it wasn't a laugh born of genuine amusement but a nervous one.

I decided to pretend I knew more than I actually did.

'Well, look . . . I know all about it.'

'Tell me, what was the family background again?'

'She came over here after the war and did various things, I think, and then set up old people's homes in the sixties in Ewell and Epsom and places like that. Then she went into hotels.'

'Yes. I can't remember the details, and I mustn't say anything that's inaccurate, but I well recall there was an awful lot of very deep unpleasantness over a couple of issues. The inference was that your mother had . . . had . . .'

'Yes? What? Had what?'

'Had used . . . look, I really can't remember all the details, and it's not really for me to say . . .'

I left a gap for him to fill but he wasn't falling for it. Silence.

'OK, so how do I contact Humphrey, then?'

'Well, look, I don't want to be unhelpful, but believe it or not, I only knew his French address about a month ago, because he turned up on my doorstep, looking all sentimental, wanting to chat about old times and he happened to be over here. Now all I can do for you, which I will gladly do, I will write to him and give him your details, and knowing Humphrey, he's quite likely to get in touch.'

'That's really kind of you. I mean, him and my mother were great friends, and I remember him very fondly.'

'Yes, well, just so that you have all the information, all the papers of Benson and Co. have long been destroyed – 1972 was a long time ago and the storage problem is vast and he didn't take anything with him at all.'

'Yes, but Humphrey being a solicitor will probably remember it all anyway.'

'Well, I doubt it. You'll find unfortunately, with all of us, as the years pass, the brain will be a bit . . .'

'Yes, but he won't have forgotten my mother.'

'Look . . . I'll do this for you. Because when he was over here, he asked me to get a book for him from the office, so I'm getting in touch with him anyway.'

After that it was time to do some more filming for *House of Horrors*. The bit where I was supposed to see how easily I could con various members of the public out of thousands of pounds. Before I could be let loose on doorsteps, however, I had to undergo one of those appalling physical makeovers you see on TV, in order to make me look like a proper salesman. Also, having been on TV for the last ten years, I needed a disguise or I might be recognized, in which case the game would have been up before it had even started. Hence the need for a haircut, a new hair colour, tinted contact lenses and a suit and tie. Ugh. The last time I wore a suit and tie was also on TV when Princess Diana died and my editor threatened to sack me if I didn't. Anyway: it didn't go too well. I visited twelve houses – all in a very moneyed part of Buckinghamshire – and failed to get as much as a sniff of a sale. I was supposed to be selling a brand-new, exciting product costing only £3,999: 'a revolutionary new building membrane for the front of your house, which is scientifically proven to reduce damp problems and add to the life of your property'. Trouble was, I couldn't stop being nice to people and therefore disobeying the instructions I had been given by Jay, the high-pressure selling expert. I came in for special criticism after one case, involving a potential connee who looked just like my wife. As a result I embarked on an extended session of mild but harmless flirting. This, said Jay, listening in on proceedings in a nearby van specially rigged up for the purpose, was a disaster. My chances of winning a sale by flirting, he said, were roughly the same as those of a one-legged man winning an arse-kicking contest. He had a point. When it came to interesting her in my extraordinary housing membrane product, she politely declined. Had we both been single, though, I'm fairly confident I could have sold her a drink. The production team want me to have another go, soon. But next time, I have been warned, I am going to have to be more forceful and manipulative.

1976–85

One minute we owned what felt like half of Surrey. The next, my mother was on benefits and warning we might not be able to afford a roof over our heads. Not for the first time, however, it turned out she had been overstating the case. In the end, she managed to rescue enough cash from the twin wreckages of the Bosham and Nonsuch Hotels – she had lost both, owing to recession, illness and lack of decent staff – to put down a deposit on a three-storey, semi-detached house in Egmont Road, Sutton. Now, finally, we were living together: my mother, brother and I, fourteen and a half years after she gave birth to me. Just like a normal family. Except that she couldn't quite shake off the business habits of a lifetime. There were rooms going spare at 20 Egmont Road. And to her, empty rooms meant the possibility of cash.

To start with, she paid off the mortgage by letting the entire top floor to tenants. An attractive (at least they were to me, aged fourteen) pair of sisters from Ireland, Rita and Kathy, were the first occupants. They made quite an impression. I can still remember the shock and awe at seeing their pink underwear drying on the banisters at the top of the stairs. You must understand: I was an overweight, greasy teenager at an all-male boarding school who hadn't got to within 3 feet of a girl, ever, let alone her underwear. So the sight of those knickers being paraded, achingly and symbolically out of reach on the top floor of our house, sent me into quite a tailspin.

It wasn't easy settling into our new life. The ugly sisters of disharmony and discord were our permanent housemates. From the off, it was familial civil war. Let's start with my mother and my brother Pete. They just didn't understand each other. Germaine Greer and Bernard Manning would have got on better. She couldn't fathom why he wouldn't get up until 2 p.m. every day, refused to get a proper job, and had a bedroom that smelt as if a dead cow had been rotting under its floorboards for several years. He, in turn, kept losing his temper when she went on about all of the above, and more. She used to blame him for everything that went wrong. In our first summer there, I developed a twitch, which meant I blinked a lot. I had no idea what caused it. But our mother decided it was Pete's fault because he teased me and so she banished him to the shed at the bottom of the garden. He lived there for a few weeks but the horrendous arguments continued. Eventually, after a few months, he took the sensible option: permanent exile, in the shape of a move to a crappy one-bedroomed place not far from Sutton station.

He made a fuss about being kicked out but he was in his twenties, to be fair. She said that he couldn't call himself a man until he set up house on his own. Then again, she may just have been after the rent from his room. She started advertising it as a room to rent before she'd even fumigated it. He made a stink about it (metaphorically this time), as I say, but he must have known it made sense. If they had carried on living in the same house someone might have got badly hurt.

My relationship with her, meanwhile, was slightly better. But not much. I had never lived with her properly, remember, so I had never been subjected to any parental discipline. And I was becoming opinionated and tactless. Our main problem was that she simply steamrollered over people who disagreed with her . . . and I used to disagree with her a lot. And I also didn't like giving way. That caused problems of the irresistible force and immovable object kind. In her world, you see, she was always 100 per cent right, even when she was 100 per cent wrong. When she ran hotels this didn't matter as she had a flotilla of paid flunkeys around her whose job it was to agree with everything she said, no matter how ludicrous, extravagant or unreasonable. But I, for better or worse, felt under no such constraints. So when she said something questionable, I questioned it. And she didn't react well to being questioned. Once, for example, she gave an unsuspecting visitor – a gas man who had come to read the meter – her life story. When she got to the bit about what a superb businesswoman she was, though, some of the facts seemed to go astray. I couldn't resist. After the gas man left I posed what seemed the obvious question. 'If you're as great at business as you make out, how come you lost everything . . . the two hotels and all the houses and all the cars?'

A bit cruel, I suppose. But what I had heard didn't quite tally with what I knew and I couldn't stop myself letting her know that. She wasn't happy. If you had jabbed Mike Tyson in the chest and called him a feeble, cissy gay-boy rapist he couldn't have reacted worse than she did. I was thrown out of the house on the spot. Not for the first time and not for the last. It was the way she used to do it that really got me, though. The way she screamed 'GET OUT OF MY HOUSE!!! NOW!!!' as if she really hated me. It used to take a week at least, and sometimes several, before her incandescent anger subsided and I was allowed to return. In the meantime I would stay with friends or on Pete's food-stained couch.

The first few times I got thrown out I found it deeply unsettling. I hadn't experienced that kind of treatment from anyone, ever, let alone my own mother. She sounded so vicious: she really seemed to mean it. On the very first ejection I was so shell-shocked I simply stood in the road crying, waiting for Pete to pick me up. I wore sunglasses to try to hide my tears. Gradually, though, I grew anaesthetized to these episodes and coped with them by learning to see the entertaining side.

One day, after expelling me yet again to Pete's one-bedroomed pit, she introduced a new tactic: use of the telephone answering machine as a weapon of strategic psychological torture. I think she may have been inspired by one of those late night psychological thrillers you see on TV. The first time she used this tactic we had just walked through Pete's front door when we realized his answering machine had a message on it. The first time we played it back, it spooked us a bit. I had never heard a voice – let alone a woman's voice, let alone my own mother's – so laden with cold, staccato venom. For some reason she left a short gap between each of her words, for effect. She sounded like a cross between Hannibal Lecter and Margaret Thatcher. 'Jonny. This. Is. Your. Mother. Speaking. Don't. Ever. Come. Round. My. House. While. I'm. Alive. Do you hear me? I. Never. Want. To. See. You. Again.'

Click. End of message. As in, end of that particular message. She wasn't done with me yet. 'Don't think you're off the hook yet, sonny,' the machine would have said, if it could talk, 'because there's more where that came from.' Sure enough, the click was followed by another gem of a message. My Mother's Revenge, Part 2. Or Return of the Mother.

'Hello? Jonny? One. More. Thing. Just. Like. Your. Sister.

Rachel. You. Know. Where. To. Go. When. The. Chips. Are. Down. Don't you? You. Fucking. Little. Shit.'

It sounded as if she was reading it from a script. As I said, at first, I found it a bit shocking and upsetting. But it didn't take long for Peter and me to build up quite an archive of these messages. We soon realized we had a unique and extraordinary piece of audio entertainment on our hands. Word got round his friends and mine that our answerphone tapes had to be heard to be believed. So people used to drop by for a listen and a cup of tea. Once they heard what was on the tapes, their mouths would drop and tea would be spilt. After a while, we became so desensitized to the variety of insults and threats she used to leave on the machine that we made compilation tapes of her greatest hits and carried them round with us, in case we bumped into someone in Sutton High Street who fancied a listen. A lot of people did.

Another bit we learned to enjoy was trying to predict who would crack first: i.e., who would weaken and say sorry or at least reopen the lines of civil communication. This led to some excellent moments. Once, when Pete was still at Egmont, he and my mother were a week into yet another not-speaking-to-each-other-under-any-circumstances cold war. One evening, for some reason, they both found themselves accidentally watching TV at the same time. After a while Pete decided to switch channels. This infuriated my mother, who had been enjoying the programme. But she couldn't say anything, of course. She knew – and she knew that he knew that she knew – that to express her dissatisfaction verbally would have meant her losing face, and the battle. So the moment he switched channels, instead of saying something, she started gesturing frantically, like a hyperactive traffic policeman. Pete, a trifle sadistically – but who can blame him – pretended not to notice. So she started making strange grunting noises, emanating from somewhere around her neck region. The inference was pretty clear: I'm Not Going To Back Down And Talk To You So Switch Back To The Other Channel, Or Else. But Pete sensed his advantage. He knew he had her riled. He also had the remote control. (They'd just about been invented back then.) He also knew she couldn't operate the TV without his help. So he carried on ignoring her. Which got her even more agitated, of course. In the end she was reduced to aggressively waving a piece of paper in his face, with the words 'TURN OVER NOW' hurriedly scrawled on it. It was a pyrrhic victory for Pete: soon after that he had to move out.

Once my mother sensed that her usual tactics – abusive answerphone messages, poison pen letters, etc. – weren't having quite the same effect as they used to, she upped the stakes. I had grown complacent: I had come to believe I was reasonably immune from her verbal slings and written arrows. There was nothing she could do to really hurt me, I thought, as I'd heard it all before. I could see it coming and knew how to cope with it. But she was marvellously inventive when it came to finding new ways to pierce my sensitivities. After a couple of years at Egmont I had (thanks to a diet of the eighties equivalent of Slimfast and cheese and biscuits) lost a lot of weight and, miracle of miracles, suddenly found I'd become reasonably good-looking, with a close circle of good friends. She knew they meant everything to me and were an essential emotional support network. So one day, when we started arguing, she brought that knowledge into play, masterfully. I had just mentioned I was going to stay with a friend.

'No you're not.'

'Why?'

'Because they hate you. Your friends. All your friends hate you.' That took the wind out of my sails. She said it so coldly, so confidently.

I suspected she was bluffing but I couldn't be sure: being eighteen didn't help.

'How . . . how do you know?'

Damn. I had shown weakness. And she knew it. She moved in for the kill.

'They told me. They hate you. All of your friends told me they hate you.'

Looking back, I now feel something close to admiration for the exquisite cruelty she displayed that day. Like a brilliant boxer,she had lasered in on my flaw and punched the living daylights out of it. At the time, I was shocked but not upset. I couldn't believe she had said what she had said. It was callous and cruel, perhaps. But I don't think she was an emotionally callous and cruel person, full stop: it's just that she always wanted to win, at all costs. Whatever she needed to say, to win an argument, she would say. I don't think she ever stopped to think what effect her words – whether written, spoken or recorded – might have.

Talking of which, she loved questioning people's mental stability. Especially her own children's. Once, after she'd had an all-guns-blazing row with Pete, she wrote me a letter. I was at school when I got it. It cheered me up no end. It consisted of a page photocopied from a dictionary of medical psychology. It listed all the symptoms that would be shown by a psychopath. At the top, she had scrawled, 'Who does this remind you of?' She had also highlighted, with a marker pen, various psychopathic traits. They included: difficulty finding stable and regular employment, unusual sleeping patterns and a disrespect for authority. Quite entertaining, really. Just to make sure I got the message she had also written, in very large letters at the bottom of the page, 'YOUR BROTHER!!!!!' Pete found it rather amusing and even ended up admitting that she might have had a point.

The boring old cliché about food and Jewish households is justified, by the way. My mother wasn't an Orthodox Jew – she never went near a synagogue in her adult life, to my knowledge – but there was one Jewish trait that never left her. Food always loomed large. She spent more time in Marks & Spencer food halls than the people who worked in them. Our fridge, in particular, was a source of great wonderment to all who saw it. Friends called it the Tardis. Like the legendary phone box, it looked a normal size. But when the door swung open it was like entering a football stadium. There were pyramids of cooked sausages, vats of coleslaw and funeral pyres of cooked chicken pieces. And that was just the top shelf.

But it wasn't just food which was plentiful at our house. After a while, beds were, too. My mother's business antennae had spotted another opportunity. The AAAAA b & b for the DHSS. For the confused/dyslexic among you, let me explain. New regulations had been brought in which meant that the Department of Social Security (DHSS) had to pay for accommodation for homeless people who couldn't get council flats. My mother quickly saw the potential. And realized that the accommodation didn't exactly have to be palatial – or, more importantly, spacious. So she set about creating as many bedrooms – or rather units – as possible. My bedroom on the first floor, which was a fair old size and therefore an ideal candidate for renovation, was the first to go. I was sent to live in the cellar, which she had extended and converted. Into my old room came a partition, and four single beds: two on each side of the flimsy new 'wall'. In some rooms she went even farther and subdivided them again, using more partitions. Pete asked her why she didn't go the whole hog and just give the guests upright coffins to sleep in; I joked that she was simply conducting research into how to split the atom. She ignored us both. This obsession with getting the maximum number of residential units out of a limited amount of bricks and mortar clearly made its mark. Pete still has nightmares about it, more than twenty years on. In them, our mother moves in with him. He goes out to the shops. When he comes back he finds she's converted his front room into four separate units and there's a bloke from the council there telling him sorry, but it's too late to do anything about it.

A few weeks after launching her new business venture, my mother made an important discovery. She realized she could do a deal with the local council which ensured she got paid directly. Previously, the rent money due to her had been paid to the DHSS tenants, who were then supposed to pass it on to her. Not surprisingly that often failed to happen and the money (and sometimes the tenants) would get lost in the bars, betting shops and off licences of Sutton. Once she struck this deal with the council, however, she had a very handy and steady stream of reliable income. As for the AAAAA bit of the equation, that was her cunning way of ensuring that she was always the first name people came across when anyone looked under 'Bed and Breakfast' in the local Yellow Pages. At first, she simply called herself 'The A & B Guest House'. That was enough to guarantee alphabetic supremacy and thus top billing. But then a local competitor called his place 'The AA Guest House'. Relishing a fight, as always, my mother retaliated by renaming her gaff 'The AAAAA Guest House'. Her competitor, perhaps sensing what he was up against, quietly threw in the towel.

Sometimes, however, the DHSS tenants were a little unruly. We once had a drunken Irish couple who – there's no delicate way of putting this, M'lud – had a tendency to go to the toilet whenever and wherever the feeling took them. It may have had something to do with drugs. Whatever: it didn't take long before the consequences became apparent, aroma-wise. Trouble was, the tenants refused to leave. So my mother decided to go nuclear. 'If. You. No. Leave. My. House. Now,' she warned them, in tones chillingly reminiscent of those messages left on Pete's answerphone, 'I MAKE you leave. You no believe me? I give you twenty minutes. If you not out, then I get you out. Myself.'

They laughed, she told me afterwards: but they weren't laughing twenty minutes later. I didn't see what happened but I couldn't fail to hear it. She went upstairs with a hammer and methodically smashed every single window in the couple's room. It made for quite a symphony. Each smash was followed by a woman's scream (the female tenant's, not my mother's). Not for the first time, I was left wondering what on earth the neighbours made of it all.

After a while she had a pretty good business on her hands. Sometimes, at the end of a particularly good week, she would wave huge wads of cash around with a slightly crazed look in her eye, telling me what a brilliant businesswoman she was and how she had 'shown them all, those fucking bastards'. I was never sure who these 'fucking bastards' actually were, but given that generous dollops of the cash would often end up in my pocket, I remember feeling rather grateful to them for spurring her on.

Soon, my mother's colonization of the house in the name of profit maximization began to know no bounds. One night I brought a girl home, late. I left her in the kitchen sipping coffee and made my way down to my cellar bedroom, as quickly as decorum would allow, to create that all-important pre-coital ambience. I immediately noticed that something had changed. All my posters had been taken off the walls and there were two suitcases next to the bed. I slipped into my mother's bedroom to find her in what had become her signature position: flat on her back, remote in hand, flipping TV channels.

'What's happened to my room?' I whispered. 'I'm with a girl!'

'Oh, sorry, darling,' she said, in a matter-of-fact way. 'I thought you weren't coming home tonight, so I let your room. Only two nights.'

I ended up sleeping in the lounge. Alone.

My mother was also, as far I could make out, sleeping alone. In fact since Dennis and Gay Edward, there hadn't been anybody serious. But she was still out there, trying to find love. She wasn't sleeping with anyone, as far as I knew, but she was certainly seeing one or two blokes every now and then. She still wanted to find love, that's for sure. And she was pursuing it with the same laser-eyed determination that she brought to all her projects. To that end, she had joined a dating agency for mature men and women. Hence the piles of papers I used to find around the house with all her potential dates' details on them. Each sheet listed a would-be suitor's personal details and sported a big tick or cross in the top right hand corner, depending on whether or not she liked what she'd read. Her vanity wouldn't let her admit that she'd joined a dating agency, though. When she brought blokes back, for dinner but not dessert, she would always make a point – too much of one – of telling me afterwards how she'd met them in the food hall at Harrods or whatever. I didn't want to burst her bubble so, in a rare display of tact, I never let on that I knew the true source of all her gentleman callers. The blokes that made it back to Egmont were all, without exception, fifty-plus, very straight, very English and had names like Charles or Roger. She clearly still had a weakness for the English Gent type. But she also wanted something a bit extra – something unpredictable and/or creative – which is why, ultimately, all the pages headed Charles, Roger et al. ended up in the bin. But it didn't seem to depress her. Her light still shone and she still had hope. And that seemingly unquenchable appetite for a project, be it financial, emotional or psychological.

Talking of the psychological, she would, in another life, have made a good military strategist. Not in terms of tactics and battle plans, but the psy-ops element: i.e. the bit that involves messing with your opponents' minds. She was certainly pretty good at messing with mine. Until I learnt strategies to help me deal with her, that is. What would have let her down at the highest military level, however, would have been her tendency to be simply too unorthodox. Actually, unorthodox is the wrong word. Make that irrational.

One day I was loading something into the washing machine when something behind it caught my eye. It was a photograph, stuck to the wall. I leant forward to take a closer look. It was Dennis, in his Household Cavalry days, all dressed up and on a horse. But that wasn't all. There were several pins stuck into the photo. A few had been driven into his head, one or two were poking out of his torso, and the rest had been planted firmly in his groin. That wasn't all. There was a wisp of something taped to the picture. At first I thought it was fluff from the washing machine. I bent forward to take a closer look and realized it was a clump of human hair. It was brown. The same colour as Dennis's. Wow. Just another day at 20 Egmont Road. I didn't know whether to laugh or be shocked. In the end I rang Pete and did a fair bit of the former. These days, I'm more inclined to the latter. I knew she was fascinated by the occult but I hadn't, until then, realized the extent of it.

The weight I had successfully shed – all 2½ stone of it – hadn't disappeared completely. It was as if it had hung around in the air and transferred itself, bit by bit, to my mother's bottom, thighs and stomach. She wasn't very tall, so it could have been disastrous. But thanks to a combination of girdles, cannily cut dark clothes and shawls, she managed to hold the worst effects of it at bay. She was prepared to go a lot farther than the clothes rack, however, in her attempts to look good. But again, as with the dating agency business, she wasn't keen on revealing her methods. One day she walked into the house with her head swathed in bandages, so I asked her what had happened. 'I am walking through Harrods, when this woman stopped me. She had very bad look in her eye. She said her husband was looking at me and she was very annoyed because he found me so attractive. So she take off her stiletto shoe, and hit me here . . .' She gestured to the right side of her face, just next to her eyebrow. '. . . and here.' She then pointed to the same area on the other side of her face.

Right. Let's get this straight, I thought. You were walking through Harrods when a strange woman with very sharp stilettos suddenly and violently attacked you, on account of her husband finding you overwhelmingly attractive. And it just so happens that she wounded you in perfect symmetry on either side of your head. But you didn't press charges. And you seem surprisingly calm about it all. Hmmm.

The extreme doubts soon hardened into 100 per cent disbelief when the bandages came off. Her alleged wounds were in fact tiny incisions that looked very much as if they had been made by a surgeon's knife. But the skin on her face was now less lined and more taut. I wasn't quite sure who she was trying to kid – me or herself – but again, wisely, I resisted the urge to blunder in with any ill-considered comments. Things went from amusing to farcical, however, when she caught me staring at her wounds/incisions one day, across the kitchen table.

'You want to know the truth?' she said.

'Aha' I thought. 'She knows I know.'

'OK.' I said.

'Well . . . it's quite shocking.'

'It's OK, I think I know, Mum. It's all right, it's no big deal.'

I braced myself for her explanation/justification. As in 'I'm a woman, I worry about getting old, etc., etc.' She has smelled my cynicism, I thought, and now she wants to regain the psychological high ground. By letting me know that she knows that I know. She pursed her lips and spoke without emotion.

'Cancer of the eyebrows.'

'What?'

'Cancer of the eyebrows. I have cancer. In my eyebrows. That is why I had operation. That is why I needed bandages.'

I sensed she needed me to say something sympathetic so I did my best. I may have said 'Oh dear, that's terrible' but I doubt it carried much conviction.

What made it even more of a giveaway was the fact that she had once been a public pioneer of cosmetic surgery: in the sixties and seventies she discovered it big time. She was singing its praises and having it done regularly a good thirty years before it became the unremarkable event it is now. In those days few talked about it openly. But she didn't care. In fact, the more people she told, the better. She posed for ' Before and After' articles in women's magazines and boasted how many parts of her body had gone under the surgeon's knife: nose, breasts, cheeks, neck, upper arms, the lot. She became quite an expert on the subject. When she wasn't having it done, she could be found reading books about it. I often found her trawling through her enormous green medical textbooks on plastic surgery. Utterly compelling they were too. I can still remember some of the pictures – men with elephantiasis of the penis, women with purple warts the size of apples on their cheeks, that kind of thing.

Despite all this, though, she stuck to her cancer of the eyebrows story. The word 'facelift' was never mentioned. As always, it was about getting a reaction. That was the way with her: when it came to getting a reaction, she was insatiable. It didn't matter what emotion it contained – sympathy or adulation – as long as it was extreme. And if it wasn't extreme enough? Well then, she would just have to up the stakes. Clearly, my reaction to her eyebrow cancer was deemed unsatisfactory. Which is why, a few weeks later, when I came home for what I thought was going to be Sunday lunch, she pulled another stunt. As soon as I walked through the door I noticed her body, in a nightie, slumped on the kitchen floor. The moment she realized I was in the house she started to move, very slowly. Using her elbows to haul herself along, she edged her way across the kitchen lino towards the oven. She was groaning and also, I noticed, had an oven glove on one hand.

'Got . . . to . . . get . . . Jonny's . . . dinner,' she gasped, inching closer to her Gas Mark 6 Everest, '. . . even though . . . dying of cancer . . . Jonny's dinner . . . most important thing. Even though . . . cancer . . . uuuuuuuurrgghhhh.'

'No please, Mum, it's all right,' I said, opening the oven door for her.

'No!' she shrieked, before launching into her routine again, the clear inference being: 'Don't worry about my cancer, your dinner is more important.'

What was it all about? If her plan was to make me feel guilty she had failed. I was more puzzled. Why go to such lengths to convince me of her health problems, real or imagined? Maybe I hadn't been sympathetic enough in the past. But then she had been drawing very deeply from that particular well for a mighty long time and there simply wasn't anything left.

Even though we had our wild ups and downs, my mother and I, we always made it up. Sometimes the sendings to Coventry lasted for weeks; occasionally months. But whenever the fracture in our relationship looked liked becoming permanent, two simple truths kept propelling us back to each other. We were tied by blood. I was her youngest son. We needed each other, I guess. With others – neighbours, customers, tradesmen – there were no such considerations. As a result, fledgling friendships or business relationships that she had formed would often end in spectacular and very permanent fashion. People would often stop me in the street and say things like, 'Please tell your mother that I think she has treated me very shabbily.' But I was never quite sure why. When I used to ask her about why these people were so disgruntled, she would come out with a stream of abuse, usually aimed at them.

I got an insight into what some of them may have been talking about one day. There was a lovely-looking girl – Wendy, I think her name was – who lived in a house whose garden backed onto ours. I fancied her like mad and I reckoned I was in with a chance. Wendy used to have the odd – in both senses – pleasant chat with my mother. I say 'chat', but it was more monologue than dialogue. It would start with my mother proffering Wendy her views on life, the universe and everything, before advising – or rather telling – her what she should be doing with her love life, her social life and her job. These mini-lectures would then end with my mother listing all her glorious achievements in the fields of business, commerce and twenty-first-century space travel. Wendy seemed to find it all quite entertaining but the unfortunate events of one Saturday night in the summer of 1984 put paid to that.

Wendy decided to hold her twenty-first birthday party in a marquee in her parents' back garden. She hired a live band and they played loud and long. Unfortunately she hadn't told my mother what to expect. When it got to past midnight and 'Hi Ho Silver Lining', my mother decided she had had enough. I knew there was going to be trouble when I saw her jaw tighten and that cold 'whatever it takes' look take hold of her face. She marched out of the house in her nightdress, got into the car and sped round to Wendy's. A drunken reveller opened the door.

'Yesh? Hello! Who are you?'

'What is going on?'

'It's Wendy's party.'

'Get her. Now.'

Wendy came to the door.

'Oh, hello!' she said.

'What is going on?'

'It's my twenty-first birthday party!'

'I hope you never live to see your twenty-second.'

Wendy retired hurt in floods of tears to an upstairs bedroom. That's one way to get the music turned down, I suppose. I never saw or heard from her again.

It wouldn't be fair to say that all my mother's relationships ended this way, however. She inspired different emotions in different people. The planets of bewilderment, hero worship, hatred and gratitude all circled her personal solar system. Lynn and Ron from number 52, who worked for her, would have lain down in the middle of the fast lane of the motorway for her if she'd asked them to. She was very good when it came to these master-and-servant-type relationships actually. I think it had a lot to do with her generosity. If she was happy with something Ron and Lynn had done she would reward them handsomely – with cash, champagne, a huge joint of roast beef or sometimes all three. The champagne option always went down well with Lynn, a Beryl Reid look alike with quite a thirst. She would often wobble in at ten in the morning smelling like a brewery and looking as if she had just been hit over the head with a truncheon. She got away with it, though, as she had perfected a good line in unconditional, hero-worshipping patter that went down a treat with my mother: 'Yes, Mrs

Wynton, no, Mrs Wynton. Cor! You are brilliant, Mrs Wynton!' Ron's weakness, on the other hand, was his other hand. He had a tendency to let it wander. Especially when there was a young girl's bottom in the vicinity. His main area of expertise was allegedly the garden but he showed a lot more commitment and ability when it came to copping a feel. My mother didn't really mind that, though. In fact she found it quite amusing. Especially since he used to turn up for work every day in a grubby, stained grey mac that might as well have had a sign saying 'Dirty Old Man' emblazoned across the back. But she did mind, terribly, when he used weedkiller instead of fertilizer on her beloved roses. Overnight, every single one of them died. It was the only time I ever saw her cry.

When casual passers-by got caught in her crossfire, it usually ended in utter, joyous confusion. One day the large ornamental concrete flower pot outside our front door got nicked. This vexed my mother greatly. She decided she would find the culprit. There was one problem, though. She was not a fan of the long, slow, painstaking forensic examination backed with a mountain of irrefutable evidence. It wasn't a case of finding *the* culprit, any culprit would do. Within hours of the crime taking place, she named the guilty man. It was the bloke down the road who owned a pick-up truck. Her reasoning was simple and, as far as she was concerned, flawless. He was the only person in our road with a vehicle big enough to put our large ornamental plant pot in. He was, therefore, 100 per cent guilty. She waited until he was walking past our house before beckoning him over. He was a rough-and-ready builder type and not the sharpest tool in the box. She got straight to the point.

'Hey, you. You stole my planter.'

'What?'

'You stole my planter.'

'I what?'

'You stole my planter!'

'What you talkin' about? I don't even know what a planter is. Wossat?'

'You no know what planter is? What you think planter is?'

'I dunno . . . sumfink to do with plants?'

'Aha! Now you talking turkey!'

'No I'm not.'

'Yes! Yes you are! Now you talking turkey!'

'No, I'm not talking turkey.'

'Yes you are! You talking turkey!'

And so on. Exit stage left, after about three minutes, a dazed and confused builder, found guilty by both judge and jury standing in session on the doorstep of 20 Egmont Road, of stealing a planter.

I made the mistake of trying to reason with my mother afterwards.

'Mum . . . you can't just do that,' I said.

'Do what?'

'Just go up to strangers and accuse them of nicking stuff, just like that, when you've no proof.'

'No proof? No proof? He owns pick-up truck for fuck's sake! He put it in truck and drive off with it! Who else done it? I know it was him. You know why I know? Educated guess! Educated guess!'

After I left university I got a job on the local newspaper: a free sheet called the *Sutton and Cheam Guardian*. The offices were only a fifteen-minute walk away so I tried living at home. It soon became clear, however, that my mother wanted me to move out. Whether this was for my own good – i.e. she wanted me to become independent – or because she wanted the extra income from my bedroom, I'm not sure. But the terms she offered were good. She would pay to furnish the entire flat herself, and there would of course be regular food parcels. It was an offer I could not refuse.

14 July 2005

This could be interesting. I am in Cornwall this week with my wife and two stepsons, trying – not very successfully – to avoid eating too many Cornish pasties and cubes of honeycomb fudge. At the end of each day I check for messages on my mobile, even though it pisses my wife off royally. She says we come down here to relax and disconnect and not fret about e-mails, texts, phone messages and the like. She is probably right but I am addicted, for better or worse (probably worse), to maintaining some kind of electronic contact with the real (or as she calls it, the unreal) world. And anyway, as I've pointed out to her already this week, this project is different. To me, this isn't work, it's life. As it happens, we've been down here six days already and I've had no messages whatsoever. But this evening there was one: from Humphrey Benson, sounding very much like a post-lunch Henry Blofeld, the BBC radio cricket commentator. He said he would love to hear from me. Good. I will call him when I get back to London.

19 July 2005

'Hello?' The tones were immaculate, clipped and female. It could have been the Queen but it was, I assumed, Mrs Benson IV.

'Ah yes, hello. Is Humphrey there? It's Jonathan Maitland.'

'Yes, he is. He's just in the garden. I'll go and get him.'

After about three minutes Humphrey came on the line.

'Well, I must say I'm very pleased to hear from you,' he said.

'And I must say I'm very pleased to hear you're alive . . . there was a rumour going round that you'd . . . shuffled your mortal coil. It's good to hear that reports of your demise have been greatly exaggerated.'

'Exactly! There are the most extraordinary rumours going around in Epsom which I pick up from time to time, all complete nonsense, like I'd gone bankrupt . . .'

'Oh yes, Nick Carstairs mentioned that I might hear stories like that,' I interrupted, 'but that they were all complete poppy-cock and bollocks.'

'Yes. Well, what really happened, Jonathan, was this.'

Humphrey then gave me his potted history, most of which I knew: left the company in Epsom, went to live in Colchester with wife number four (whom he's been with for thirty-five years) and set up a new firm in Ipswich, did very well, moved to France four years ago.

'Tell me,' he said, once he'd finished, 'I see you're in films. You're not a reporter or anything, are you? You're not going to write all this down?'

'Quite possibly, yes . . . I'm doing a book about my mother, you see, and I'm trying to find out some of the things that went on. And you're a pretty key player . . . I mean, she used to talk about you all the time, didn't she? And she was clearly very fond of you.'

'Ha ha ha. Well, let me tell you, I never dealt with your mother after I left Epsom but she was the most amazing client I ever had. I can tell you that.'

'I was just wondering if you could tell me a bit of other stuff too, because I've been told there might have been some trouble about a will in the sixties or seventies and I was hoping you might remember something but I don't know if you're in a position to tell me.'

'Well, I will tell you everything I know but it's difficult, really. Perhaps you should come over here. Get the train to Dinard, we can pick you up, it's a two-hour drive . . .'

I interrupted again. 'Yes, I may come over but in the meantime . . .'

'Ha! You sound just like your mother! Brushing me to one side, as usual. Carry on, Jeeves!'

'I just wanted to know what you knew.'

'Well, I am seventy-five and a half and my memory is not what it was.'

'OK, but I just wondered if you knew anything about a bloke called Stern and his will, or why the old people's homes were closed down.'

'I really have no idea.'

'Is that "I really have no idea" because you've conveniently forgotten? Or because of some lawyer–client confidentiality thing? Or because we're entering choppy waters? I mean, can't you tell me anything?'

'I'll tell you what I recall about my times with your mother. She was always scheming and trying various dodges. I can't remember what they were, but she would always say, "For Christ's sakes, Humphrey, give it a go."'

'Ah yes. Like with the Mercedes thing, when they sued her and she pretended to be a halfwit.'

'Oh yes. Yes, that sort of thing. Yes, I know the one. Marvellous. Very good. Ha! Yes, she was always ducking and diving, she had a very original mind, she got up to schemes which I could never have dreamt up myself, because I have no imagination anyway, and she used to ask me what I thought and I would usually say, "Well, it's extremely dodgy, but give it a go".'

'What? Dodgy as in illegal?"

'Good God no! Dodgy as in "Well, it'll never work but you might as well try." I'm a solicitor, for God's sake!'

'That's what I mean! Can you remember what the most dodgy thing she got up to was?'

'No.'

'Oh dear. OK. Are you still tall and flamboyant, by the way? That's how I remember you and I just want to make sure I've got the right picture of you in my mind.'

'Hold on, I'll just ask my wife.'

There was a short, muffled, off-telephone chat followed by laughter.

'Yes! Oh yes! Tall and flamboyant, that will do.'

'Good. Well I'll let you know if I find anything out.'

'Yes, do. Nothing would surprise me. But I mean . . . she was a bit of a crook.'

'Really? How so?'

'Well, like I said, I really can't remember. But let me ask you . . . has your family got any old files lying around, anything relating to that time?'

'Almost certainly not. But I'll make enquiries.'

'I'll tell you what, though . . . I want to say this, Jonathan, seriously, if you can get your father, if he's still alive, to give a bit of information on what she got up to, it might well trigger my memory.'

Hmm. Did Humphrey know more than he was prepared to say?

21 July 2005

From: jmaitland@xxxxxxx
To: mmaitland @xxxxxx
Date: July 21 2005 16.34
Subject: Documents

Hi – had an interesting chat with Humphrey Benson the other day. He seemed to remember nothing, but I'm not sure if that was for real, or convenient. He asked if we had any documents left over from those days. Don't suppose we have, have we?

Cheers

J

25 July 2005

have just made a second, unsuccessful attempt at trying to see Graham and Linda, the couple who currently own the Nonsuch Park Hotel. If I ever get round to visiting them I don't expect I'll see many guests as Graham's phone manner is not exactly warm and inviting. He couldn't have been less welcoming if I'd told him I was from the Highways Agency and was about to build a six-lane motorway through his hotel dining room.

ME: 'Hello, I called last week about coming round to have a chat. About the old owner, Mrs Wynton. I'm around tomorrow, midday. Does that suit at all?'

GRAHAM: 'Not really.'

ME: 'Right. OK. The day after perhaps?'

GRAHAM: 'That's when I do my macro run.'

ME: 'Right. You're doing some kind of marathon, are you?'

GRAHAM: 'What?'

ME: 'A macro run. What's that? Thirty-five miles or something?'

GRAHAM: 'Makro is our supermarket. That's the day I take the car and stock up on stuff for the hotel.'

ME: 'Oh. OK. Look, why don't I just come down . . . when-
    ever.'
GRAHAM: 'You can try looking in, I suppose. Goodbye.'

There are two possibilities here. The first is that Graham knows
something about the events of the sixties and seventies and is
being deliberately obstructive because he feels disapproving or
awkward. The second is that he is Epsom's answer to Basil
Fawlty and I am being paranoid.

26 July 2005

I spent most of this evening trying to get hold of the manuscript of the book my mother wrote. It was a bit of a kerfuffle. I followed my brother's instructions and got in touch with the tenant of his flat in Hammersmith. He, I hoped, would lead me to the prize. It was, Maurice said, somewhere in his flat's rooftop storeroom. But it wasn't that simple. For a start, Maurice's is no ordinary flat. By that I mean that it's not a standard one bedroom conversion job or in a nice, small, easy-to-get-to block. It's part of a vast complex of more than 500 flats and shops, roughly the size of three Buckingham Palaces. And although each flat does indeed have its own storeroom, all of which are on the building's huge roof, you have to be a bit of a Dr Livingstone to find the one you are looking for. Unfortunately, the tenant of Maurice's place wasn't too clued up. He didn't, he said, know exactly which bit of the roof I should be looking on. He also wasn't sure whether the key he was giving me was the right one. So I spent the next hour trying to work things out. Not easy. It was like doing an assault course. Up there on the roof, about 800 metres above street level, I got excellent aerial views of most of London. But I also found that there were hundreds of small storeroom doors to choose from, each with numbers on them. The numbers related to all the different flats in the block. But they weren't grouped together in any logical order. And there were no signs guiding you. The numbers on each door were so small you had to go right up close to see them. And the roof, which was the size of a football pitch, was covered in huge rubber-clad pipes, wooden beams and metal staircases. That meant vaulting, climbing and tightrope-walking my way across. One hour later I was considerably dirtier than I had been when I started, but also able to tell Maurice's tenant that I had, finally, located the correct storeroom. The key he'd given me, however, was the wrong one. Finally, half an hour later, having returned to the caretaker's office on the ground floor, I had got the right key, gone back up, and was finally where I wanted to be: inside the storeroom to flat number 301. And a few pounds lighter. The shed was filled with shelves lined with legal reference manuals, textbooks and dictionaries. It felt and smelt as if no one had been there for years. It was very dusty and I was coughing a lot. Maurice had told me to look on my left just as I went in, but I couldn't see anything with 'The Death Sentence' written on it. There was one file that caught my eye: it said 'AAAAA Studio accounts 1984'. I had a quick look. It showed a profit of £8,472. Not bad. Then I saw a luridly bright orange file, the type we used to have at school, with the metal clampy thing inside. At the front was a photocopy of an article from a newspaper. It was the *Daily Mail* of 6 June 1978, and it was about someone called Dom Robert Petit-Pierre ('The Church of England's leading Exorcist'). Ah yes. Brother Dom. He was a priest called in by my mother to get rid of the ghost which, it is said, haunted the Bosham Hotel. Gay Edward, with his Celtic sixth sense, reckoned the ghost was usually to be found hovering at the end of my mother's bed. 'It's here! I can feel it!' he used to exclaim.

'Really?' my mother would retort, her hair standing on end at his sheer perceptiveness. That was when she called in Brother Dom. He used to wander the corridors of the hotel wearing a dark hood, chanting and swinging an incense-filled lamp – thereby frightening the staff far more than the (alleged) ghost ever could. On the next page, after the article about Brother Dom, was just what I was looking for. It was typewritten and had Tipp-Ex smears on it.

```
          'SHOULD THERE BE ANOTHER TIME'
              Or: 'The Death Sentence'
                  Non-fiction.
                                   Bru Wynton
                                     1.9.77
```

Bingo! What treasures – or otherwise – lay within?

27 July 2005

Last night, as somebody once sang, I didn't get to sleep at all. I spent most of it reading my mother's not very thinly disguised autobiography. Maurice called it 'a novel' but she described it as 'non-fiction'. It was neither: it defied categorization. It was a cross between a spoof Barbara Cartland, the world according to Bru Wynton and a soap opera. There were events and people I recognized, but it was hard to work out where real life ended and my mother's florid imagination took over. I guess we would have to call it a novel, in the end, albeit one closely based on her own life. When Maurice mentioned the book in his e-mail it brought back memories of her writing it: she bashed it out on a typewriter in the kitchen at Egmont Road at the end of the seventies, after a succession of people had told her, 'You should write a book, you know.' At the time, she had great hopes for it. She sent it off to several publishers but, despite her claim that many of them felt it was definitely the best book they had ever read, it never got published. I assumed it had been lost but Maurice – good on him – had, unbeknown to me, been looking after it all these years. I'm very glad he did. I lapped it up. It was like looking at our family history from the wrong end of a telescope.

The lead character in *Should There Be Another Time* was someone called Alexis. That, I seem to remember, was the name of the scheming, bitchy, Joan Collins character in *Dynasty*. Alexis, according to the opening paragraph, was:

> ... not a classic beauty. Her face was a striking combination of her Spanish mother's auburn hair, fiery long-lashed brown eyes, and her French father's fresh skin and aristocratic features.

Hold on a minute. That can't be my mother, then. Her parents were as Jewish as gefilte fish and matzos. But Alexis clearly was my mother, as the next paragraph found her:

> Whizzing along at 50mph in a red and black Mercedes ... once you hit the dual carriageway you unleash the monster at top speed and let the music uplift your soul and make your spirits soar like a flock of birds in full flight.

Goodness me. Further confirmation (not that it was needed) of Alexis's true identity came at the bottom of page 1:

> Men were fascinated by her ruthlessness in business and yet there was an aura of warmth and excitement about her ... her apparent aloofness only made men keener to possess her.

Then came an insight into the heroine's state of mind at that particular moment, i.e. in her red-and-black Mercedes:

> There were no doorbells here. No phones ringing. No staff barging in with silly questions, no senile old patients

demanding attention. As the shining chrome of the highly polished car kept catching the headlights of oncoming cars like falling stars, she felt on top of the world. She had everything – except love!

Alexis, it turned out, was at a turning point in her life:

To divorce or not to divorce. That was the 64 dollar question. Essentially sensuous, she felt utterly frustrated with her hard working but extremely dull husband whom she met and married when they were both in the Air Force, aged 19. Harry was a good looking man, well built and intelligent, but his mind was occupied only with thoughts of food, sleep and money.

I smiled when I read that last bit. Food, sleep and money – three of my biggest preoccupations. Whoever came up with that saying about the apple never falling far from the tree was definitely on to something.

Anyway: it soon became pretty clear who each character was based on. There was 7-year-old Jason, Alexis's youngest son, who was at boarding school. He had two older brothers, Martin and Paul, and a sister, Rita. Then there was Daizy, Alexis's 'personal maid', who was:

slightly mentally deficient . . . but with a heart of gold . . . pale faced, plain and wheezy, following the removal of one of her lungs.

Daizy had apparently been abandoned by her parents and 'left to rot in the basement of the local convent'. The Mother Superior had sent her along to Alexis's old people's home, in the hope that she might find work there. Wow. This could be a film! It raced along and was quite readable, in a Harold Robbins meets Jackie Collins meets Mills and Boon kind of way. Here on page 8, Alexis is simultaneously taking a bath and contemplating a divorce from her first, Harry, while the radio plays an exotic tune:

> As she swayed in the warm scented bubbles, her heart beat with a savage thirst for life and love and excitement too long submerged, now just waiting to erupt like a rumbling volcano. Visions of romance, passions untold and Prince Charming swept irresistibly through her mind and heart to the sexy rhythm of the music. 'I can't stand it! Tomorrow!' She promised herself. 'I will go and see the solicitor in the morning and start the ball rolling.'

She does just that. But Harry doesn't want to play ball. He wants to stay married. They have a big argument at the London Hilton. She gets into her Mercedes, thinking 'How do I get away from this loathsome brute?', and drives at speed into the iron railings bordering Hyde Park. Some of it, then, was clearly based on fact.

She goes into hospital to be patched up by a good-looking doctor and then, a few months later, finds herself in court. It is the day of the divorce. Enter Derek Winters, an ex-copper and private detective, who has been assigned by her tall and flamboyant solicitor to look after her. By page 20 he is telling her: 'You are a real woman and everything I've ever dreamed of. Marry me, Alexis!'

They get married. Alexis 'took great delight in polishing and grooming her new husband'. But soon, she notices, he is getting 'possessive, angry and jealous'. To make things worse, Alexis's ex-husband, Harry, keeps dropping in on them. So Alexis decides to find him a new wife. One day Dolores, a dark, attractive woman 'wearing a mini skirt and a trifle too much make up' turns up, wanting a room. Alexis redirects her to Harry's place, telling her: 'If you play your cards right, he might marry you.' Two months later, Harry and Dolores are married. It sounds fanciful but it is, in fact, 100 per cent true. I've seen my father only three or four times in the last twenty years but on each occasion he and his second wife, Doreen, have told me the story of how they met. And it was just as my mother had written it.

By page 23, despite a clearly vigorous sex life, which she went into in some detail, and which I read through gaps in my fingers, Alexis and Derek were fraying at the edges. As she puts it: 'She felt cheated, conned. His persistent self styled James Bond image was beginning to get on her nerves.' Poor old Derek then cops dozens of pages of extremely harsh criticism.

Then came the bit – journalistically speaking – that I was looking for. Bottom of page 32, top of page 33.

The months of speculation about the future of one of her businesses came to an end, as was expected. The postman delivered a registered letter one morning informing Alexis that the licence for the nursing home was being withdrawn. Although the action had been anticipated, it did not mitigate the shattering blow. Financial ruin stared her in the face . . . Derek tried to advise, but he could not quite understand the chain of events that had led to the predicament. She tried discussing the situation with him but it was futile and he did not grasp the situation.

And that was that. No more detail, no more context, no more explanation. But then what did I expect? This orange file was the last place on earth I could hope to find clear-eyed, objective, revealing information about my mother.

There was plenty of stuff about her health, too. She described, very plausibly, being diagnosed with breast cancer and the treatment and operations that followed. But again, it was hard to know where fact ended and fiction took over. According to *The Death Sentence*, she didn't just have breast cancer – not that you can ever 'just' have it, of course – she also had cancer in her skull, spine and brain. This, according to the narrative, meant that doctors had to remove her ovaries and her adrenal glands. I'm no expert, but the moment you get cancer in your brain, isn't the referee of life pretty much blowing the final whistle? She also wrote about the agonies of deciding how, and whether, she should tell her children about her illness. This didn't quite square with my experience, I have to say – i.e. finding out about it from the front page of the local newspaper during a school French exam.

And then there was Edward. As in Edward the gay head waiter. I thought he was just a fling: a bonkers dalliance, something to take her mind off her disastrous marriage(s) to Dennis/Derek. According to *The Death Sentence*, however, her affair with Edward – 'Simon Bailey' in the book – was a full-blown, life-affirming love match. In the book they meet for the first time when he comes for a job interview at her hotel, 'The Belair' in Bosham. It was clear from the way she described him where they were headed: and it wasn't the wine cellar.

She eyed him surreptitiously. He was in his late thirties, under six feet tall, athletic build, dark, with exquisite features. Eyes rich green velvet with long black silky lashes. His dark beautiful hair sprinkled with silver, strong white teeth gleaming in the slight tan of his face.

Oo-er. Within pages, Alexis is 'curing' him of his homosexuality and they are in love. In the end, though, our heroine decides that, because she is dying, she must send him away. She does not want to put him through the agony of seeing the woman he loves die.

'Simon . . . It's finished! You and me.' She gestured. 'It's all over!'

He stared at her with the same incredulous look that she saw on his face the night he was told she had cancer. He was stunned. 'What's brought this on for God's sakes?'

The action then moves to a hospital corridor, where they say their last farewell.

She felt the pain welling up inside her heart as she clung to him desperately. Her fingers dug deep into his arms. He bent down and kissed her. His eyes were full of love. 'Let me look at you!' he whispered as he gazed at her, memorising, etching in his mind every line of her face, the look in her eyes, even the tears. 'Alexis,' he whispered again and her heart stood still, numb as stone within her. She saw the same green loving eyes, awestruck, the same passionate mouth, vainly searching for words. For a moment they stood staring silently at each other, too stunned even to feel pain.

'Simon!' she said in a trembling voice. He looked away and the line of his jaw tightened as he turned to go. She put her hand out but suddenly he was gone. As his footsteps got fainter down the hall she knew that a part of her went with him too. 'Goodbye my darling,' she cried softly but he could not hear her. 'I love you . . .'

Blimey. I think she really loved him. But off he went, neverthe-less. To Peru, of all places. Don't laugh. It must have been quite touching. If it actually happened this way. Which it may have done.

28 July 2005

I drove down to the Nonsuch Park Hotel this morning. It was the first time I'd been back in more than thirty years. The first thing that struck me was how little it had changed: the flag-poles my mother had put up in the mid-seventies were still there, as was the big white sign stuck to the front of the building. Even the last seven digits of the phone number – as displayed on the sign – were the same as in the mid-seventies. The only clue that a third of a century had passed since I was last there was the Web address, which had been stencilled on to the bottom of the hoarding. The second thing that struck me was how depressing it looked. But that may have had something to do with the fact that it was a filthy, damp, slate-grey day. It wasn't very busy: there were just two cars parked outside. I assumed Graham, the Fawlty-esque manager, was still on his Makro run. I peered through the glass front doors but couldn't see anyone so I let myself in.

God. It seemed so much bigger when I used to live here. Oh, look . . . there's the bar. On the left, just as you come through the front door. It's exactly the same as it was when Mum put it in. Slightly cheap and tacky mahogany wood effect. Looked good and classy then, but horribly dated now. That's where I saw those two blokes, in full make-up and see-through black chiffon shirts, snogging each other with tongues and grinding their pelvises against each other the night I nipped down in my pyjamas for a cup of cocoa. And here's the main office. Hold on, it's only three steps from the front door. It's all a bit cramped. I remember it being so much bigger than this. In my mind's eye this place was the size of an ocean liner. Why do things always seem so much bigger in your memory?

The office was empty. Round the corner to its left I saw a television screen. ITV2 was on, showing a repeat of the *Jerry Springer Show*. In front of the TV I could see a pair of legs, clad in a shiny black tracksuit, attached to a very big belly. I rang the bell marked 'Service'. The belly's owner got up in a flash. 'Hello,' I said, hazarding a guess. 'Are you Graham?'

He was indeed. And I take it all back. That stuff about him being Epsom's answer to Basil Fawlty, I mean. He was as nice as pie. He'd clearly been eating a few, too: his face was a perfect circle. In person, though, he was as warm as his phone manner was terse. Yes, of course he'd show me around, he said, no problem.

First stop, the bedroom where I was born. When I was older we would use this room as a sitting room. But now it's full of bits of wood and building tools and the walls are being stripped. Again, so much smaller than I remember. 'We're making it into an en suite,' said Graham. 'Everyone wants en suite these days.'

'Er . . . can we see the room next door?'

And here is my mother's bedroom.

'Ah, this is where my mother pretended to die on me once.' Graham looks at me as if I have just suggested that we nip under the covers together.

'Die . . . no . . . we were just playing a game, that's all.'

'Oh.' Graham looks mildly confused.

It is a dowdy, bog-standard bed-and-breakfast room with a white nylon counterpane on the bed, a Corby trouser press on the wall, and – of course – a small table with tea- and coffee-making facilities. Where are they? Oh yes. There they are, next to the kettle. Those little corrugated plastic cartons of artificial milk and two sachets of biscuits. I cannot believe that stuff went on in this room. The past is indeed another country, because this is not the place I knew. It was so vibrant and vivid then. Now, it's drab and mediocre. Maybe memories only come in Technicolor.

Before I went I asked Graham how long he'd owned the place. Since 1990, he said. Had he heard anything about the previous owner? The woman who owned it in the seventies?

'Only that she made it into some sort of gay retreat.'

Yes, but did he know why it had changed from being an old people's home?

'No idea. Jan might know.'

He beckoned over the cleaning lady, who was picking up ash-trays in the bar. But she didn't know, either.

'You might try the people I bought it off . . . Mr and Mrs Capewell. They still live locally. They had it for about thirteen years before I bought it off them. They might know. They're in the phone book.'

29 July 2005

This morning I wrote a letter to my sister and this afternoon I had another go at scamming members of the public, for the TV show.

The letter was difficult: how to reopen communications with someone you haven't spoken to for eighteen years? After all, 'Hello, how are you, what have you been up to' doesn't really seem appropriate, does it? My sister and I, and indeed both my brothers and she, appear to have gone down the same route that our mother did with her siblings: we have let a family disagreement harden into a bitter argument which, in turn, has become an implacable, long-term feud. I don't want to go into details; suffice to say it was about money. People tell me it's a shame that I haven't seen or spoken to her since 1987, but I don't see it that way. Having a relationship with her was just always . . . very complicated. I can't say more than that. This book is about my mother, not her. Now, however, I have a reason to get in touch with her. I hope I'm not playing with fire.

Dear Rachel
  I hope you're well. I am writing a book about our

*mother which I thought you might be able to help me
with. I am trying to work out why Twin Gables, the old
people's home that our parents ran in the mid sixties,
closed down. Apparently it had its licence to operate
taken away by Epsom District Council. I have been in
contact with Maurice about this and he isn't sure exactly
what happened but you were older than him at the time
so I thought you might be a better bet. There is a clue,
which might help: Maurice says he remembers seeing a
letter from the family solicitor, Humphrey Benson, about
one of the residents, an old bloke named Stern.
Apparently there may have been one or two 'issues' about
him and his will. Ring any bells?*

   *I know this is all rather sudden and out of the blue and
a bit weird but I didn't want to leave any stone unturned.*

   All the best

   Jonny

After that it was off to a posh bit of Buckinghamshire again
to play Dick Turpin for the TV cameras. This time I was more
successful. I visited twelve homes and actually managed to get
two people – both women and both in their sixties – to sign up
for four grand's worth of my rubbish product. A turnover of
£8,000 in one afternoon: not a bad (half) day's work. I have to
admit that I felt a small but undeniable sense of elation when I
got both the ladies to sign the contract agreeing to have the
'work' done. (Once I'd left their houses, I was back within minutes to explain what had gone on and to ask their permission for
the secret footage to be shown on TV.) It worked just as Jay, my
scamming Svengali, said it would. My first victim was a gentle,
attractive woman who used to do all the admin work at a local
primary school. She was just too nice. Churchgoer, pillar of the

community, not an ounce of malice. I sensed her weakness straight away so I told her that her sofa didn't go with her curtains. 'Ooh . . . not sure about that sofa,' was the exact phrase. 'Oh really? Gosh. Why?' After that it was like shooting fish in a barrel. I rather callously instilled the requisite bit of fear in her – 'If you don't have this work done, Madeleine, there is a good chance that you will need to spend twice what you spend with us on having your home put right, in less than five years' time' – and then pulled the age-old con trick of pretending that if she wanted a special, one-off 25 per cent discount, she would have to sign up today, or it wouldn't be available ever again. As I say, I felt no shame when she signed on the dotted line, just a rather satisfying sense of achievement. I can see – almost – why people do this kind of thing for a living.

30 July 2005

From: Mmaitland@xxxx
To: jmaitland@xxxxx
Sent: 30 July 2005 21:06
Subject: Re: more feud for thought

There is someone else you might try calling who might have some interesting information but I don't know what kind of response you'll get. Judging by the response I got, it might not be good. To explain . . .

I used to be mates with a guy called Peter Bruinvels, an ex Tory MP. I bumped into him years ago in the street and then tried to track him down afterwards by ringing his Dad, Stanley, who lives in Dorking. He was an estate agent then but he's since retired. On hearing my surname, Stanley immediately changed his tone from friendly to irked: 'Oh no! Not the Melman from the Twin Gables old people's home in the 1960s?' It's just that Mr Stern had estate agent links, too: his family were the Stern and Parsons people. Bruinvels Senior might have known him . . . and can maybe shine a little bit of light on the darkness. Just a thought.

I was irate that our parents' misdemeanours – perceived or otherwise – were being taken out on me. As an investigative, on-the-spot journalist, it shouldn't be too difficult for you to work out what happened – or what didn't. All you need to do is find out the full name of a Stern who lived – and quite possibly died – at Twin Gables, in the sixties. Then, I think, it would be a very good idea to get hold of a copy of his will.

There is another thing. I remember, years ago, our uncle (Dad's brother, Max Melman) confiding in me about one of the ruses our parents used. When people would come to Twin Gables to visit their elderly relatives, Dad would produce a shit-covered mattress and ask for compensation. The visitors, who could not disprove the allegation and who, in any case, were too embarrassed to argue, would nearly always produce a cheque on the spot.

Maurice

31 July 2005

I'm getting more and more nervous and uneasy about this whole thing. Granted, I have made pitifully slow progress in my investigation. And I have found no smoking gun – indeed, there may not be one. But each new scintilla of information increases the feeling that, at the end of it all, I am going to find something that isn't very pleasant at all. It is beginning to dawn on me that there is a very real possibility that my parents' moral compass may not have been set to the same coordinates as other people's. It feels disloyal, somehow, investigating them. But I have gone too far to stop now. That e-mail yesterday – about the shit-covered mattress – was a line-in-the-sand moment for me. If it's true, that is. They shouldn't have done that. But if they were prepared to go that far, what else did they do?

The call I made this morning only reinforced my feelings of unease. I phoned Stanley Bruinvels, as recommended by my brother. He is eighty-four now and his memory isn't what it was. But once I'd given him a few names, dates and locations the fog started to clear. 'Well, there was some trouble, involving an old people's home in the Sutton, Epsom area, I remember that now. It was all a bit nasty, I think. You know, to do with money and all that. But I can't remember what happened, as I am a very advanced octogenarian. What did you say your name was again?'

Right now, if I am to make any progress, I need to find the details of the Mr Stern who stayed at Twin Gables in the sixties. Once I know his full name I will then, presumably, be able to get hold of his will. I also need to speak to his relatives. But how am I going to do that? I have no idea which part of the country to start looking in or whether they will want to talk to me. And there are more than a hundred Sterns living in London alone, for a start. I could play Stern Lotto and phone every single one, I suppose. It may yet have to come to that. Failing that, I could go to Probate House and check out every single will left in the name of Stern, as Maurice said. But it is a very common name. I might have to book another week's holiday off work.

I phoned Mr Capewell this morning, too: the bloke who bought the Nonsuch Park Hotel from my mother in 1976 when it was going dead cheap in the sales. He wouldn't tell me how much he paid for it but when I said to him, 'Cor, you must have got yourself a bit of a bargain,' he didn't dispute it. At one stage I thought I might be on to something. He had found a huge pile of papers in the attic one day, he said, during a clear-out, and it was all quite interesting. I held my breath. I needn't have. It was newspaper cuttings about the hotel becoming a haven for homo-sexuals.

1985–6

There's a hoary old Jewish joke about a Yiddisher mama whose son is drowning. She runs along the beach crying, 'Help! Help! My son the lawyer is drowning!' In another version, the lawyer is a doctor. Yes, another whiskery old Jewish cliché: but one based on fact, if my experience is anything to go by. When I was growing up and my future career prospects were mentioned, my mother's response was always the same. Doctor or lawyer. Or maybe a barrister. I knew I was never going to travel down the medical route, though. I had no interest or aptitude in things chemical/biological/physical. But the law thing was always a possibility. Which is why I did it at university. This encouraged her greatly. But one day, soon after my course ended, I decided the law was not for me. My tutor at London University had recommended that I go to one of those ceremonial dinner things that all trainee barristers have to attend. You had to go to twelve, I think, before you could qualify as a junior barrister, or something like that. Normally I would need no encouraging whatsoever to eat twelve dinners. But after seeing what went on at the first one, I decided to give the other eleven – and the entire profession – a miss. The whole thing reeked of snobbery, smugness and vested interests. It was so Establishment, like a cross between the masons, public school and the police force. I toyed with becoming an actor or comedian. Then I opened the *London Evening Standard* and saw an article about some university graduates who'd been given jobs as trainee reporters by ITN. There was a picture of them in the ITN newsroom. They looked delighted. I was jealous. But liberated. I now knew exactly what I wanted to do. It wasn't until 1985, however, that I finally got my break. I had spent the previous two years working for the *Sutton and Cheam Guardian*. Newspapers, I had gleaned from talking to people in the business, were where all TV reporters started. But after a while on the *Guardian* I started to lose my mind. It was so boring. And petty. I used to spend all week writing rubbish stories about how local people were pissed off with the youths hanging outside the McDonald's in Sutton High Street. Or how Banstead Hospital was holding a fund-raising day for its neo natal unit. Then, if I was lucky – lucky! – I would be sent along to interview the widow of some poor bloke who'd died in a car crash. There were one or two perks, though. Namely food and music. I set myself up as the paper's music critic and so used to get sent vast quantities of free LPs from record companies. Also, every so often, restaurants that advertised with the paper would qualify for a 'Wine and Dine' feature. This was basically an advert for the restaurant in question, masquerading as an unbiased editorial review. But someone had to write it: and that someone was usually me. Wonderfully, that involved me and a friend eating a very large and very free meal at the establishment in question and then writing sycophantic rubbish afterwards, regardless of whether the meal was any good or not. 'Bhajis like cricket balls . . . the best selection of starters since the men's 800 metres Olympic finals . . .' That sort of thing. As for the issue of journalistic ethics . . . I couldn't give a toss. As far as I was concerned, there *was* such a thing as a free lunch and it was very enjoyable indeed. But not enjoyable enough to keep me working at the *Sutton and Cheam Guardian*. All I could think about was escaping. Preferably, into the BBC. But all the BBC could think about, it seemed, was rejecting me. I was turned down at least five times. I applied to be a tape operator at Radio Bedfordshire. A programme assistant at Radio Manchester. Then, one day in June, I went to my mother's for lunch. There was a letter addressed to me on the mat with the BBC logo in the top left-hand corner. I knew what it was. I had applied for a place on one of their trainee radio reporter schemes. I mentally prepared myself for rejection and then tremblingly set about opening the envelope. I looked for words like 'regret' and 'unsuccessful' and 'unable to offer you a place', but to my amazement found myself staring at 'pleased' and 'successful' instead. I ran into my mother's bedroom. She was, as always, on her back in her nightdress with the remote control in her hand. 'Mum! Mum! Mum! I've done it! I've got into the BBC! Fuck! Fuck! I'm in! I'm in! BBC! BBC!'

'I knew you would do it! I knew!'

She was thrilled. Genuinely. Doctor, lawyer? The BBC was a perfectly acceptable substitute. From that moment on our relationship attained some kind of equilibrium. I had, in her eyes, succeeded. She was dead proud. The day she heard my first ever broadcast on national radio she was so proud she couldn't contain herself. I had done a report from Bristol – where I'd got a job on the local radio station – which had been played on the Radio 4 *PM* programme. It was about a bunch of students who'd disrupted a speech by Enoch Powell at Bristol University. The moment she heard it she tried to ring up the BBC to congratulate me. She got through to the main switchboard in London and started haranguing the operator: 'I want to talk to my son! He has just been on Radio 4! Put me through to him immediately!'

Now that we weren't living together, there were far fewer arguments. I was at a safe distance – i.e. Bristol. I had learned how to tolerate, humour and indulge her. There was give and take. Mainly, she gave and I took. Then again the AAAAA Guest House was doing pretty well so she could afford to. She bought me cars and clothes and gave me loads of cash. There were new projects in the pipeline too. She had noticed how dating agencies for men and women of a certain age and status, i.e. hers, were doing rather well. So she started her own. In late 1985, whenever I came home – usually at weekends, and usually for an enormous Sunday lunch – I would notice piles of brochures, leaflets and headed notepaper for her new business baby, 'Supper Club Exclusive', lying around the house. She actually made a bit of money out of it before finally losing interest.

One Sunday in the late summer of 1986 I turned up to find her looking quite different. She had made an effort, for the first time in ages, to look good. She had make-up on and a new hairstyle. She'd got her leopard-print top out of the cupboard. As soon as I walked through the door I knew someone else was there, someone whom she wanted to impress. It was the way she greeted me. Whenever she wanted to put on a show for someone, she would always go a bit over the top. She thought she was being warm and welcoming but it always seemed a bit forced and artificial, as if she were trying too hard. And on this occasion she was trying very hard indeed. There at the kitchen table was a short bloke in his fifties wearing – uh-oh – shades, even though it was lunchtime. The style was mutton dressed as lamb: the hair was bouffant and he was dressed entirely in black. He had Cuban heels on his shoes but when he stood up to greet me, I noticed, he was still a bit of a short-arse. He also had a tall

glass on the table in front of him, filled to the brim with a clear
liquid that I assumed was water. His face was small and leathery
and when he took his shades off his eyes looked small and puffy.
He spoke in one of those slightly fake mid-Atlantic drawls. My
mother introduced us as if he were a visiting dignitary rather
than the DHSS tenant he actually was. 'Jonny, darling . . . this is
Vic. He is a guest here. I have invited him to have lunch with us.
He is from Canada. He is a professional singer. Listen.'

She made a point of cocking her ear towards the sitting room,
where the stereo was playing. It sounded like Frank Sinatra. A
bit.

'It is Vic!' said my mother excitedly. 'Look!'

She held up an album cover that had been lying on a kitchen
unit next to a humongous, sizzling joint of roast pork. There on
the cover was a picture of Vic, *sans* sunglasses, trying to look
alluring. The album's title was something like *Vic Franklin Sings
Sinatra*. I tried, for my mother's sake, to look and sound
impressed.

'Hello,' I thought to myself. 'What, exactly, are we getting
into here?'

1 August 2005

I wish all this stuff hadn't happened so long ago. Once upon a time there were official records that would have revealed exactly why Twin Gables closed down. But the key institutions of that time are now defunct. Epsom District Council, according to an e-mail from Maurice, withdrew my parents' licence to operate old people's homes in the late sixties. But that administrative body went the way of all flesh some time in the seventies, to be replaced by Epsom and Ewell Borough Council (EEBC). Hoping against hope that EEBC might have records going back that far, I rang their archivist, a nice lady called Susan. No luck there. But she suggested I try something called the Committee for Social Inspection, a government-backed body that regulates old people's homes and has the power to close them down if necessary. Getting warm! I rang the regional office in Guildford. They told me they couldn't help but that I should ring head office in London, who definitely would. But head office in London told me they couldn't help either, and that I should ring . . . the regional office in Guildford. The people I'd gone to in the first place. I was the ball in a game of bureaucratic ping-pong. Tricky business, this investigative journalism. Every time

I think I might be about to take a step forward, I take two strides back.

My other avenue of investigation involves trying to find out more about this Stern character. Ideally, I want to see a copy of his will and talk to his relatives. But before I do that I need to know which Stern I am looking for, as there are loads out there. So, to that end, I have tried another tactic. Hamish, my childhood friend (and discoverer of my dark school-uniform-in-the-holidays secret), is now, you may recall, an estate agent. It was he, or rather one of his colleagues, who managed to put me in touch, eventually, with Humphrey Benson. Given that Mr Stern was an estate agent, or members of his family were, and given that Hamish is one too, I thought he might be able to help. So I rang and asked him whether he knew any Sterns.

Alas: he was familiar with the company name but knew none of its people. He did have a suggestion, though: 'Why don't you try *Who's Who*?'

Good idea. Why didn't I think of that?

A few minutes later I was on to a helpful-sounding lady called Vicky, the *Who's Who* head of marketing and publicity, sucking up like mad. I was stuck at home with monstrously painful toothache, I said, truthfully enough, and couldn't make it down to the library. Did the current edition of *Who's Who*, or the historical version, *Who Was Who*, have entries for any well-to-do landowning types called Stern? Vicky said she would get back to me. I am not giving up. There must be a way.

2 August 2005

The following plopped into my electronic mail box this morning:

From: Vicky at Who's Who
To: jmaitland@xxxxxx
Sent: August 2 2005 09:34
Subject: Stern

Hi Jonathan

The only Stern I've managed to find is Sir Nigel Edward Stern of Stern and Parsons Farms. He was in Who's Who but he died in Jan. 2004. There are no living Sterns in Who's Who with connections (as far as we know) with Stern and Parsons. Sorry we can't help more.

Best wishes

Vicky

Far from being unhelpful, Vicky at *Who's Who* may have given me my most valuable lead yet. I got on to the Net and keyed the words 'Sir', 'Nigel' and 'Stern' into Google. Precisely six taps on the keyboard after receiving her e-mail, I was on the World Wide Web and a website called www.thePeerage.com: 'A genealogical survey of the Peerage of Britain as well as the Royal Families of Europe.' And there, in front of me, were the details of a bloke called Sir Nigel Edward Stern, who had indeed died in 2004. Thank the Lord for the Net. WWW: Where Would We be without it?

After a handful of clicks on relevant parts of the website, I had established the following: Sir Nigel Edward Stern, the bloke who was listed in *Who's Who,* had a brother and a sister. They were called Mark and Gillian. Stay with me, this is going somewhere. Both were born around the time of the First World War and would now, I realized, be well into their eighties. The website said that they were both alive. But it also said that the site had last been updated in 2004, so they might not be alive any more. The Stern children, Gillian, Mark and Sir Nigel, were the offspring of someone called Edward Jolliffe Stern, who died – I noticed, with a slight quickening of the heartbeat – in 1964. Hmm. Could Edward Jolliffe Stern be the man my brother was referring to, the one whose will might hold the key to this whole thing? Certainly, the timing seemed to be about right: 1964 was when my parents would have been in the middle of running their old people's homes empire. I knew what I needed to do next. I had to track down his relatives and talk to them. I clicked my mouse on the name of Gillian Stern, his daughter. Hey presto, I was through to another page of the website, giving her details. She, it said, had married someone called Mr Nutting. They had two children. One was a boy called D. A. Nutting. He, I worked out, would be about sixty by now. He would also be Edward

Jolliffe Stern's grandson. But how on earth do I track down D. A. Nutting? The website gave no address or phone number, just a date of birth. Well, I could try directory enquiries, I suppose. Nothing ventured, nothing gained. But which city to try? Might as well start with London.

'Yes,' the operator tells me, 'there is a D. A. Nutting listed in south-west London. Shall I put you through?'

Yes please. A woman answers. She sounds like she is in her thirties.

'Hello, I'm trying to track down a Mr D. A. Nutting. Is he there?'

'No, I'm terribly sorry, he does own this house, but he actually lives in Milton Keynes. May I be of any help?'

She's a nice person. And helpful. Glory be!

'Yes, you might well be, actually. I'm a journalist, and I'm writing a book and I was trying to track down a lady called Gillian Stern . . .' The woman at the other end of the line interrupted me. 'Yes, that's Grandma. She lives right next door to him.'

I tried not to sound too triumphant. Early days yet.

'Aha! Would that be the Gillian Stern whose father, Edward Jolliffe, passed away sometime in the sixties?'

'Yes. That's right.'

'Superb! Not for Edward, obviously, but . . . is Gillian, you know, all present and correct, marble-wise?'

'Oh yes, she's right on the button. But it might be best for you to call my father first, as she keeps getting these calls from people trying to sell her things and it confuses her. She might think you're one of those and give you short shrift.'

'You're absolutely right. I do television programmes about these people, I know what they're like. Could I possibly have your dad's phone number?'

'Of course.'

Excellent. This is quite exciting, I thought. I rang the number she gave me. A posh-sounding woman answered, her voice echoing around what sounded like a very substantial hallway indeed.

'Hello, Middle Creek Hall?'

It turned out that Mr Nutting was abroad. But he would be coming back late the following night before jetting off again. I could catch him then if I was lucky. I think I might be making headway.

Winter 1986

It didn't take long before I realized that Vic, my mother's Canadian crooning friend, had got more than just his feet under her table. The clues were there for all to see: one afternoon I turned up to find his records, of which there appeared to be many, spread out all over the sitting-room floor, along with several cheesy black-and-white photos of him trying to look sexy/mysterious/enigmatic. The sound of his not-that-bad-at-all Frank Sinatra impersonations filled the rooms and corridors of 20 Egmont Road, 24/7. And his sunglasses, I noticed with a slight start, were on my mother's bedside table. Wow. He'd gone from guest bedroom to master bedroom, in under three weeks. She'd lost a tenant but gained a lover. And he wasn't just enjoying the bedroom facilities, either: the drinks cabinet, we soon realized, was also seeing a lot of him. One day Jane, who is married to my brother Pete, took advantage of a rare event: the fact that the ever-present glass of transparent liquid wasn't in Vic's immediate custody. She took a sip.

'Uuurgh' she spat, literally. 'It's vodka.'

'We all have our problems,' said Vic.

He was, it transpired, a very thirsty man indeed. It must have been all that singing. And the only thing that could quench his thirst was Smirnoff. Soon we were all referring to him as Vic Vodka. I didn't mind his drinking habits: he seemed to handle the stuff pretty well. Mind you, on the rare occasions when he took off his shades, his eyes were now looking puffier than vol-au-vents. I wasn't bothered about his intentions or anything like that. I was just pleased my mother had found someone she liked. It couldn't have been easy for her, letting him get that up close and personal. By now she was sixty-two, and hadn't had a run out on the playing field of love for ages. She clearly harboured one or two doubts about him, though. 'What is he doing with me? I'm no spring chicken . . .' she used to say. But she put those embryonic misgivings to one side, because he had brought her back to life. She was making an effort with her appearance again. She was wanting to go out for meals. She would attempt to start 'interesting' (and rather painfully contrived) conversations whenever I came home, in the hope that I would be impressed with her new man, and vice versa. They looked pretty good together and made, I thought, a reasonable pair. They were both small, liked music (mainly his) and were good at talking about themselves for long periods of time.

But it didn't take long for my mother's newly sailed ship of romance to hit its first rock. One night they went to see Vic Vodka's parents, who lived in nearby Beddington. Out of the blue, just before they left, Pete and his wife Jane turned up and asked whether they could tag along. This, in hindsight, was a bad decision. Pete and Jane have always found humour in the excessively banal. Vic Vodka's dad, apparently, fell into this category. The evening turned into a scene from the excruciating Mike Leigh play *Abigail's Party*, only worse. Vic Vodka's parents, who lived in a very modest two-up, two-down place, had made quite an effort. They had also taken the obvious precaution of going to the off-licence beforehand. And my mother, wanting to impress them, had taken along an expensive bottle of brandy. Vic, as you would expect, launched into the bottles like a greyhound out of the traps. But on this occasion, Pete and Jane joined him. Quite a few drinks in, Jane asked Vic Vodka's dad what he did for a living.

'I put things in boxes . . .' he said in a flat monotone, reminiscent of E. L. Wisty, Peter Cook's comedy tramp-on-a-bench. He wasn't being ironic. '. . . and then I put those boxes on top of other boxes.'

'And how long have you been doing that for?' enquired Jane, trying not to snigger. Dangerous territory here.

'Thirty-seven years.'

'Thirty-seven years? God! Doesn't it get a bit boring?'

My mother started to shift uncomfortably on the floral-patterned sofa. Strangely, for one who so often took a sledgehammer to social conventions, she wanted this occasion to pass off as unremarkably as possible. But she sensed the way things were going. Vic Vodka, meanwhile, bristled.

'Well, I suppose it could be more interesting,' volunteered Vic Vodka's dad.

'Yes, I suppose it is quite a long time, to be putting things on top of other things, thirty-seven years.'

Oh dear. Jane started laughing. And so did Pete. Vic Vodka told Jane to shut up. She called him an alcoholic. He told her she was flat-chested and needed silicone implants. Not the 'More tea, Vicar?' type evening my mother had planned. She was distraught. She always wanted, and was used to getting, control. And this evening, the one that she had planned as a showpiece, had spun out of hers.

That evening didn't spell the end of her relationship with Vic Vodka, but it certainly signalled the beginning of the end. I didn't hear how it finally fell apart from her: she had too much pride to volunteer that information herself. I soon heard what had gone on, though. Vic, on one of his many visits to the local pub, the Green Man near Sutton station, had started becoming over-friendly with the barmaid there. My mother became suspicious. She had, after all, lost husband number 2 and number 3 to a barmaid, when Dennis started his affair with Sue. My mother followed Vic Vodka down to the Green Man one night, saw what was going on and confronted him. He didn't deny it. She slung him out. It was over, not too long after it had begun. And Christmas was coming.

3 August 2005

I thought I might be making headway . . . but I'm not. Not nearly as much as I had hoped, anyway. I rang up Mr D. A. Nutting last night. He, if the Stern family tree which I've drawn on my notepad is correct, is the grandson of Edward Jolliffe Stern. The Edward Jolliffe Stern who might, just might, be the mysterious 'Mr Stern', whose will was referred to in that letter Maurice saw all those years ago. I could be opening a can of worms here, I thought, as I dialled Mr Nutting's number. And how do I explain my reasons for calling, exactly?

I needn't have worried. I had barely got past the apology stage, i.e. 'Sorry to ring you out of the blue and all that . . .', when the very headmasterly-sounding Mr Nutting cut in. 'Look. It's gone ten o'clock. And I'm watching the news.'

I was halfway through trying to say 'I'm really sorry to disturb you' (I think I'd got to 'sorry') when I heard a click. And then silence. And that was that. Technically, he'd hung up on me. But he was right – it was late. So I tried him again this morning. And he was in a better mood.

I explained I was looking into my mother's activities during the sixties and that there may have been an incident that may have involved the Stern family. Did the names 'Melman', 'Maitland' or 'Twin Gables' mean anything to him?

'Absolutely nothing at all.'

Oh dear. Was he sure?

'Absolutely.'

He confirmed that Edward Jolliffe Stern was indeed his grandfather and that he had passed away in 1964. But nowhere near Twin Gables and certainly not in the presence of a Mr and Mrs Maitland. All was not lost, however.

Mr Nutting – who wasn't overly helpful, but certainly not rude, just brisk and businesslike – told me that his grandfather, Edward Jolliffe Stern, had a brother. He was called John James Stern. And he may well have died in the sixties. But he wasn't sure, as he knew very little about him: that side of the family had always been a bit of a mystery to him. And it was no use talking to his mother Gillian about all this as she was well into her eighties and wouldn't have a clue what I was on about. Fine, I said. I thanked him, and he was gone. And so was I. To my shed at the bottom of the garden. And www.thePeerage.com.

Here we go. He's right, you know. Edward Jolliffe Stern did have a brother. John James Stern, known as 'Jack'. And he died in 1968. Again, the timing seems to be just about right. Could this be the Stern that holds the key? I wonder.

Christmas 1986

Has become more and more significant in my mind, every year that passes. At first, it seemed as if our Christmas festivities were going to be like all the others. One enormous turkey, so big it needed a crane to deliver it, and several bitter rows, which meant that there would only be two (or at the most three) family members to tackle it. This year's roll-call of misery was much the same as previous ones. My mother wasn't speaking to my sister. So she wasn't invited. Pete was invited but he had a huge argument with my mother on the happy day itself, about whether he wanted stuffing and broccoli and carrots, or just stuffing, and why was he being so ungrateful and . . . which culminated in him storming out of the house and slamming the front door behind him, not long after he'd arrived. That just left me and her. We'd had plenty of Christmases like this before, so I wasn't too upset. But there was something very different about her this time. On previous occasions like this, despite the family traumas, she had been alive, edgy and alert. But now there was a noticeable lack of life. Not the slightest hint of a smile or spark of joy. Usually, even at her most irrational and unpredictable, there would always be a laugh or a cackle at some stage. OK, it may have been induced by someone else's misfortune, but better to have *freude* at someone's *schaden* than no *freude* at all, *n'est-ce pas?* I had never seen her like this. And I could not work out why. As I ate my Christmas lunch, alone, she sat in the other room staring into space, saying nothing. Maybe she was upset about the argument she'd had with Pete. But in years gone by, after an episode like that, she would have been on the phone leaving abusive messages for him or ringing up one of her sisters to slag him off. I tried to cheer her up but it had no effect. She seemed preoccupied. That evening I left her in her bedroom while I watched TV in the sitting room. Towards midnight I heard a strange sound coming from the partition doors that separated the two rooms. I turned the TV down so I could listen better. It was the sound of glass tinkling against glass. I knocked on the door but there was no reply so I slowly slid the partition doors open. She was sitting on her bed, watching the TV screen. But it was blank. There was a bottle of brandy on her bedside table which was seven-eighths empty. She didn't even drink. She was desolate. I closed the doors slowly and quietly and went back to watching the television. It was just a passing phase, I thought. Soon she will have a new project and the vim and vigour will start seeping back into her.

The next day I had to go back down to Radio Bristol. I had been roped into doing some news-reading shifts over the Christmas period. She said goodbye bleakly, absent-mindedly and, for the first time ever, without a trace of emotion. She just seemed to be somewhere else.

4 August 2005

John James Stern – could he be the Stern I'm after? – had two children, so www.thePeerage.com tells me. One of each. But both, if alive, would be rapidly approaching their nineties by now. And neither of them had children, annoyingly. So this afternoon, I am going to do what Maurice advised me to do all along and visit Probate House in central London, where they keep a record of every will ever made. I may find nothing of interest. It may be that Maurice's memory is playing tricks on him. But John James Stern's will, I feel, is a stone that should not be left unturned.

5 August 2005

Probate House is an anonymous-looking office building on High Holborn. So anonymous that I have walked past it on the way to work every week for the last seven years without even noticing it. Funny how something can be under your nose for so long and you don't even know it's there. When you enter the building you get your bags checked and you then have a choice of two main destinations: WILLS DEPARTMENT to your left and COURTS to your right. I turned left, went through some brown wooden swing-doors, and found myself in the middle of a large room with lots of tables and shelves. It looked and felt and sounded like a municipal library. There were about half a dozen people there, clicking away on computers or leafing through documents. The shelves were all lined with identical, heavily bound leather books, each the size of encyclopedias, with an index on the spine. I picked one up. The label read '1987: War–Wyt'. I opened it. On each page there was a list of around twelve names. Next to each one there was a small amount of information: the date of death and the address where that person died. I quickly found the book I wanted. It was labelled '1968: Smi–Swa'. I leafed through it hurriedly and got to Stern. There were several people of that name who had died that year. But here is the óne I'm looking for. Yes, this is the one. John James Stern. He died on 12 November 1968 and his address was 357 London Road, Ewell, Surrey. That's the address of Twin Gables . . .

I went over to the main counter and told the bloke standing behind it that I wanted a copy of John James Stern's will. He asked me for 5 pounds and told me to come back in an hour. I paid him the money and nipped into the *Tonight* office just round the corner, to kill some time. I was informed that I was being sent to Prague, soon, to do a programme about badly behaved Brits who hold their stag night parties there. Someone asked me whether something was wrong. 'No,' I said, 'just a bit distracted, that's all. Nothing serious.' I found myself tapping my fingers on one of the desks at work, looking at my watch. Still twenty-five minutes to go. Fuck it, I thought, I'll go back and wait there.

When I re-entered the wills room there was no one at the counter. But there was a bright yellow folder on it with 'STERN' on the label. I looked around. There was no one there. I opened the folder. There were two photocopied pieces of paper in it, stapled together. I took them away with me and left the folder on the table. I went out into the street and began reading. This is what the first sheet of paper said:

I, JOHN JAMES STERN of 357 London Road Ewell in the County of Surrey HEREBY REVOKE all Wills and Testamentary dispositions heretofore made by me AND DECLARE this to be my last will.

1. I APPOINT HUMPHREY THOMAS BENSON and BRUCE MEREDITH CARTER both of 147 High Street Epsom in

the County of Surrey Solicitors to be executors
of this my Will.

2. I DEVISE AND BEQUEATH all the real and personal property whatsoever and wheresoever to
which I may be entitled or over which I have any
disposing power at the time of my death unto
BRURIA MAITLAND of 357 London Road Ewell aforesaid the wife of Irving Bernard Maitland
absolutely.

3. ANY Executor or Trustee hereof who shall be
engaged in any profession or business shall be
entitled to charge and be paid all usual or professional or other charges for work or business
done or transacted by him or his firm in relation
to the trusts hereof including therein any work
or business which he might as an executor or
trustee have been required to do or transact in
person.

IN WITNESS whereof I have hereunto set my hand
this 24th day of October one thousand nine hundred and sixty five.

Then, at the bottom of the page, there was a final paragraph.

SIGNED by the above named Testator as his last
Will in the presence of us both present at the
same time who in his presence at his request and
in the presence of each other have hereunto sub-
scribed our names as witnesses.

Next to this paragraph were three signatures. One was J. J. Stern. Then there were the two witnesses. The first one was E. M. Wright, whose address was given as 355 London Road, Ewell, Surrey. Beneath his name was the word 'retired'. The second was S. J. Robertson, of 357 London Road, Ewell, Surrey. He also gave his profession as 'retired'. On the second piece of photocopied paper it said this:

In the High Court of Justice

The District Probate Registry at Lewes

BE IT KNOWN that John James Stern of 357 London Road Ewell Surrey

DIED there ON THE twelfth DAY OF November 1968 DOMI-CILED IN England

AND BE IT FURTHER KNOWN THAT at the date hereunder written the last Will and Testament (a copy whereof is hereunto annexed) of the said deceased was proved and registered in the District Probate Registry of the High Court of Justice at Lewes and that administration of all the estate which by law devolves to and vests in the personal representative of the said deceased was granted by the aforesaid court to HUMPHREY THOMAS BENSON and BRUCE MEREDITH CARTER both of 147 High Street Epsom Surrey Solicitors the executors named in the said Will.

And it is hereby certified that an Inland Revenue Affidavit has been delivered wherein it is shown that the gross value of the said estate in Great Britain (exclusive of what the said deceased may have been possessed of or entitled to as a trustee and not beneficially) amounts to £18,557-19-0 and that the net value of the estate amounts to £18,390-17-0 and it is further certified that it appears by a receipt signed by an Inland Revenue officer on the said Affidavit that £2,227-6-0 on account of estate duty and interest on such duty has been paid.

DATED THE twenty third DAY OF May 1969

Finally, at the bottom of the page, above the words 'District Registrar', there was a signature that I couldn't quite make out. It looked liked A. Hosking. I got in the car and drove home as quickly as I could.

6 August 2005

Those two pieces of paper told me quite a few things I didn't know. Here goes. Mr Stern made a new will, in 1965, aged eighty-three. It had the effect of cancelling all his previous wills, if there were any. He made and signed this new will while he was being looked after by my parents at Twin Gables. The will was witnessed – or at least signed – by two other residents of Twin Gables at the time, Mr Robertson and Mr Wright. For the will to have been legally valid, both would have had to have been in the room at the time Mr Stern signed, and actually seen him put pen to paper. Interestingly, however, the two witnesses had – apparently – different addresses. Mr Wright's was given as 355 London Road, while Mr Robertson's was 357 London Road. But the full address of Twin Gables was in fact 355–357 London Road. So, in reality, the two witnesses lived at the same place. But someone clearly had the idea of making it look as if they were less connected than they were. Presumably so as not to arouse suspicion. After all: wills are usually witnessed by family, close friends or legal officials, not two old geezers who happen to be in the same old people's home. It smacked of things being done in a hurry, without the knowledge of Mr Stern's family or friends. In this new will, Mr Stern left absolutely everything he owned to my mother. Not a penny went to his relatives. He died four years later. His estate, after tax, came to more than £18,000.

On the face of it, the document I recovered from Probate House proves nothing. It may have been that Mr Stern left everything he had to my mother willingly. But there are some deeply troubling aspects to this. And there are some very important questions which need answering. Given that he was eighty-three when he made this new will, was he mentally capable of appreciating exactly what he was doing? If he wasn't, then the will would have been legally invalid. But there is a lot more to this than just legal niceties. Why did he suddenly change his mind and decide to leave everything he owned to my mother? Was any pressure put on him? And what did his relatives think of this? Did they even know about it? Why didn't any of them witness the signing of this new will? And what, exactly, happened to his money in the end? Did my mother claim it all?

Looked at from one angle, it stinks. An 83-year-old man makes a new will and just happens to leave everything to the owner of the old people's home in which he is staying. And then dies in her care, three years later. Put it this way: as an investigative reporter, if I came across a story like this, cold, I would be licking my lips. The fact that this story has my own mother at the centre of it makes me even keener to find out exactly what went on. But I am a bit scared. What if it turns out she did something bad? As her son I think I might feel somehow partially responsible. Even though I had no way of knowing what went on at the time. Then again I may be getting ahead of myself. Innocent until proven guilty and all that. First, there are people I need to speak to. The (alleged) witnesses to the will, Mr Robertson and Mr Wright, will no longer be with us. But

Humphrey Benson is very much alive. And he told me to call him back if I came up with anything specific. I have now, Humphrey.

Then there are the two children of John James Stern. Looking at my Stern family tree I see that his son, Edward Stern, would now be ninety-one. And his daughter, Joan Stern, eighty-nine. The trouble is, I have no idea whether they are still alive or how to contact them. But I have a good lead: Mr D. A. Nutting, the headmasterly bloke I spoke to on the phone the other day. He had no idea what I was talking about but I know he has an elderly mother, Gillian. Gillian Stern. She is in her late eighties. I know she is alive. And she is the niece of John James Stern. Perhaps she knows what went on? And if not, might she know the whereabouts of his two children? Before I call her, however, I need to send an e mail.

From: Jmaitland@xxxxx
To: Mmaitland @xxxx
Sent: August 6 2005 12.34
Subject: Discovery

Maurice

I hope you're well. Sorry not to have been in touch for a while. I read our mother's autobiography, as you suggested, and it was extremely illuminating/entertaining/revealing. I'm not sure how much truth there was in it, however: a grain, a seed, or a tree.

Talking of which, I have made what appears to be a slightly disturbing discovery. I did some research on the net and found that there were two Sterns connected to the Stern and Parsons company who died in the 1960s. One of them was called Edward

Jolliffe Stern and he died in 1964. The other was called John James Stern, and he died in 1968. I went to Probate House, as you advised, and dug out a copy of John James Stern's will. It turns out that he made a new one in 1965 while he was resident at 357 London Road, Ewell – i.e. Twin Gables. Under this revised will he left everything – absolutely everything he owned, which came to about twenty thousand pounds – to our mother.

To be honest this has taken the wind out of my sails a bit. I feel deeply uneasy about it and a bit shocked. It may be that nothing untoward went on. But it doesn't look very good on the surface, I have to say. Clearly there are some calls to be made and some questions to be asked. I am going to call Humphrey in France, as he is named on the documents as an executor of the will. And I will do my best to track down John James Stern 's children, of whom there are two. The trouble is, one was born in 1914, the other in 1916. And neither appears to have had children themselves. I will of course keep you posted. I feel sick. It's all rather disturbing.

All the best

Jonny

7 August 2005

I called Gillian Stern this morning. She sounded rather frail, not surprisingly, and had difficulty making sense of what I was talking about. I got straight to the point.

'I saw a copy of your uncle's will the other day, John James Stern, that is, and it said that my mother was the sole beneficiary. I thought that was quite interesting . . .'

'She's what, you say?'

'My mother was the sole beneficiary, the sole person to benefit . . .'

'From somebody's will?'

'Yes! Your uncle's! Which I thought was a bit odd, possibly. So I wondered if you knew anything about it.'

'No . . . no, I don't.'

'Were you close to that side of the family?'

'We weren't what?'

'Close! You know, did you know John James very well?'

'Lord, no. We knew him, a bit, but that was all. We called him Jack actually. Jack Stern. Everyone did.'

'Right. Uncle Jack.'

'Yes, Uncle Jack.'

'Right. Well, I am trying to track down his two children, Edward and Joan. Have you any idea . . .'

'He's dead.'

'Who is?'

'Edward. Jack's boy.'

'Oh. When did that happen?'

'I don't know. I can't remember. I can't remember which year. No. I can't remember.'

'Oh dear. Well, don't worry. What about Joan? Do you know where she lived?'

'Yes, she's in a home somewhere. But I don't know where.'

'OK. She's eighty-nine now, I believe?'

'Yes, two years older than me . . . Joan, Joan . . .'

'When did you last see her, by the way?'

'Who?'

'Joan, your cousin, Joan Stern.'

'I haven't seen her for years. Oh, actually . . . I tell you what, you might ring up my sister-in-law, she might know. Hold on a second.'

I could hear movement at the other end of the line. Then Gillian told someone to look in a phone book. I could make out the sound of a young, female Australian voice reading out a phone number three digits at a time. Gillian then repeated those numbers, but in the wrong order every time. In the end the young woman came to the phone and told me the number herself. I asked Gillian how old her sister-in-law was.

'Oh, she's much younger than me. She's eighty, I think. Or maybe eighty-one.'

I thanked Gillian again, hung up and immediately dialled the number for her sister-in-law. Another call, another Stern. A pin-sharp, cultured voice came on the line.

'Is that Elaine Stern?' I asked.

'Yes.'

Off I went again. Name, job, project, Jack Stern, his will, my mother. Did Elaine know anything about this? Had she heard anything about it, over the years? No, she hadn't. But it all sounded 'rather peculiar'.

'It is, a bit,' I said. 'But what's happened to Joan Stern, Jack 's daughter? Do you know?'

'Joan's been in a mental home for the last fifty years. So she'd be no good.'

'What? So she's completely incapable of rational thought?'

'Oh yes.'

'Oh my God. I don't suppose she married, did she?'

'Oh no.'

'What about her late brother? Did he?'

'Oh no.'

'Right . . . Is there anyone who can help, do you think?'

'Oh yes, there is someone who, I am sure, would be hugely helpful, who knows the family backwards, because I am useless and I can't even remember the names of my own grandchildren, and that is Jean. Jean Stern.'

Oh Lord. Not another one. The Stern family are playing pass-the-parcel with me.

'She is my cousin and she's very spot-on. She is the family historian and she is the mother of the present Lord Waverleigh and she is absolutely wonderful and she just knows everything that they're all doing, or not doing. Let me give you her telephone number. She's lovely.'

'So are you. Thank you.'

We ended our conversation by trying to work out how Jean, my next Stern, was related to Jack. But it was so complicated we gave up. We agreed it didn't really matter, though. As long as she'd heard of him, had met him and knew who he was, she was a good person to call. According to Elaine, she qualified on all three counts.

So: time for a recap. John James Stern, or 'Jack', as he was known to his family and friends, left everything to my mother. He had two children, but one of them is dead and one has been in a mental home for the last fifty years so she probably didn't know what was going on at the time. None of the various Sterns I've spoken to knows anything about Twin Gables, Mrs Maitland or a kerfuffle involving Jack Stern's will. The trail has not yet gone cold, however: there is another Stern to call.

8 August 2005

From: Mmaitland @xxxxx
To: Jmaitland@xxxxxx
Sent: August 8 2005 12:56
Subject: Discovery

It's more than slightly disturbing, actually. It's absolutely disgraceful. At this stage, I suppose, we should still be trying to weigh the situation up and not come to hasty conclusions . . . but a picture of events is coming together and it is not a very savoury one. My feeling is that what happened was 100% untoward. J. J. Stern was a lovely, senile, deaf old man with glasses and a hearing aid.

By the way, I am off to Finland now, for a translator's congress. Maybe you should pause for thought too and decide whether you want to carry on with a book that throws up some deeply unpleasant things from the past. It will not exactly leave our family to bathe in reflected glory.

Maurice

From: Jmaitland@xxxxxx

To: Mmaitland@xxxxxx

Sent: August 8 2005 14: 56

Subject: Discovery

The most worrying thing about your e-mail was the description of J. J. Stern. I remember doing a course module in the Law of Wills when I was at London University. And they always made a big point of saying how dodgy it was, legally and morally, when someone who was senile/deaf/old/bonkers suddenly changed their wills. Worryingly, there was nearly always foul play involved. More on this . . . as TV reporters are wont to say . . . as and when we get it.

As for the book: I have thought about this a lot. And I'd be lying if I said that you didn't have a point. I feel a bit uneasy, setting it all down in print for anyone to see. So far I have justified it to myself in a rather glib way by simply saying that 'I've started . . . so I'll finish.' But there is a lot more to it than that.

I have been wanting to write a book about our mother for years. Hers is, and was, a remarkable story, even without 'the shenanigans', as we shall provisionally call them. I also love writing, as you do: and anyone who does craves good stories. So it would be very hard indeed for me to know that all these great stories exist, without writing them down. Now that this other stuff has started coming to the surface, I can't just leave it out – that would be dishonest. What's more, it's good therapy for me. Not that I ever thought I'd find myself saying something like that, let alone believing it.

And anyway: some good's come of it. We are talking to each other again, after several years.

Have a nice time in Finland . . .

Jonny

Early January 1987

I didn't think much about my mother's strange behaviour over Christmas. I thought it was just a phase she was going through. I didn't think there was anything wrong either when I got a phone call one day, just after I'd finished reading the news on BBC Radio Bristol. It was her.

'Jonny? Where are you?'

'I'm at work! Where else would I be?'

'What about your dinner?'

'What about my dinner?'

'It's on the table. Your dinner is on the table.'

'What?'

'Roast pork. You came in, you said you wanted dinner. So I made it for you. Why do you say you want dinner, then you not eat it? It's been on the table for two hours.'

'But, Mum . . . I'm in Bristol. I haven't been anywhere near your house for days. You're in Sutton, I'm in Bristol. I'm a hundred and fifty miles away. I never asked for dinner.'

'But it's on the table.'

'OK, thank you. Speak soon.'

I rang Pete and told him that she'd definitely gone bonkers this time. She was hallucinating, I told him. We had a laugh and thought nothing more about it.

12 August 2005

have a confession. That letter I wrote to my sister, Rachel. I never sent it. We haven't spoken since 27 February 1987, and I felt it was just a bit sudden, a bit brutal, to reintroduce myself into her life, just like that.

The reason the rift happened in the first place, by the way, was money. Ironically, it was about a will. But I've been thinking about this. After more than eighteen years of not talking – almost a fifth of a century, for God's sake – any reintroduction is going to be difficult. And now that this 'stuff' has floated to the surface, my reservations have ebbed away. This Stern business has given me the final impetus to try to re-establish contact. I left a message on Rachel's answerphone this morning explaining that I wanted to see her and why. She left a message on mine saying that it would be wonderful. I am going round to her house tomorrow morning at ten o'clock.

13 August 2005,
10.05 a.m.–10.42 a.m.

had never been to my sister's house before. She lives in Banstead in Surrey, about 5 miles from the Nonsuch Park Hotel. I actually had to ask directions from a postman once I'd found my way to Banstead High Street. All sorts of thoughts went through my head as I drove down to see her. How would we handle it? I'm not big on grand displays of physical affection so I was dreading one of those 'Let me hold you and give you a hug for five minutes while we weep silently'-type scenarios. Should I bring up the argument, the thing that caused all the problems between us, eighteen years ago? Would she? What if she didn't want to talk about what I wanted to talk about? What if she had no idea about all this Stern stuff?

I always think the same thought whenever I drive down that way and it popped into my head, right on cue, as I turned down Rachel's road. Apparently, 80 per cent of people end up living within a 5-mile radius from where they were born. That applies to Rachel, I thought. And to Pete. And me – almost. How nice to be normal and part of the mainstream.

She lived in a small, semi-detached, cottage-type place in a quiet road. I let myself in through the front gate, walked down a small front garden and went to the only door I could see, which was at the side of the house, to its right. I turned to face it and knocked on the door. To my right, as I knocked, 3 yards down the alleyway, there was a wooden door. It led, I presumed, to the back garden. I could hear dogs yapping behind it. I looked at the door in front of me again. There were two handwritten signs on it. Both were in blue felt-tip pen and looked as if they had been scrawled in a hurry. One said NO CALLERS UNDER ANY CIRCUMSTANCES UNLESS BY PRIOR ARRANGEMENT and the other BEWARE OF THE DOGS. By this time the yapping had got louder and I could hear a female voice trying to calm things down. The big wooden door leading to the garden opened slowly and a woman came into view. I didn't recognize her. She was short, dumpy, had black hair and a pale complexion. She was wearing a black cardigan, a skirt and no make-up. She reminded me of our Turkish cleaner.

'Jonny.'

It was my sister. I started babbling a bit.

'Rachel . . . blimey. I didn't recognize you. It's been quite a long time, mind you. Eighteen years . . .'

'Don't I get a hug?'

'Yes, why not.'

I felt myself stiffen and leant forward but managed to avoid full body contact. I kissed her on the cheek and we lingered in an awkward position for a few seconds, like a still photograph of two wrestlers grappling with each other. It was then that I realized who she reminded me of. My mother. Our mother. Physically, bodily, the exact dimensions. I felt surprised. I don't know why, but I was.

She let me into the house. It smelt of dogs and fags.

'Let's sit here, shall we,' she said, pointing to the kitchen table.

'How many dogs have you got?' I said.

'Three. A woman in my position needs three dogs, you know. Guard dogs. I live on my own, you know. I get all sorts of people trying it on. And those rotten plumbers and builders, I had a really bad one the other day trying to rip me off.'

'That's funny . . . I do television programmes about that kind of thing.'

'I know you do.'

I studied her face more closely. It had become wider and fuller since I last saw her. She looks nothing like me, I thought, but a lot like Maurice. Her eyes were alive and kind. I had expected them to be sad and bitter but they weren't. They had good reason to be. She had suffered the most vindictive bit of mental cruelty it is possible to imagine, courtesy of our mother. Several years ago, after a particularly bad row, our mother told her that she was not, in fact, her real daughter. That she had been swapped at birth with someone else's child. This was an outrageous and appalling lie and my mother knew it at the time: she was making it up in order to wound Rachel as much as possible, which, of course, it did. The film fans among you may recognize where my mother got her inspiration from. In *The Omen*, a small boy, Damian, turns out to be the Devil. His father, Gregory Peck, then admits to his wife that their real son was in fact stillborn and that he was swapped at birth with another child, who grew up to be Damian. It's no coincidence that I watched *The Omen* with my mother the night before she pulled her stunt on Rachel. She actually tried it on me first: with tears in her eyes, she started telling me about her so-called 'secret'. I told her to stop being stupid, laughed and pointed out that she was simply repeating the plot of the film she had just seen. If I'd known she was going to cause her daughter so much unnecessary distress I would have been a lot harder with her.

'So. You're writing a book about Mum,' said Rachel. 'I've made some notes for you.'

'Thanks, that could be interesting. Yes, she's always been an interesting person, when you look at her life, I think.'

'Yes. She was different.'

'Yes, she was different. But I am also beginning to worry that she may not have had a clear take on the difference between right and wrong. I'm worried she may have done one or two things that she shouldn't have. Like the Stern business. Mr Stern.'

'Well, I don't know about that . . . is that the builder?'

'No. He was a bloke who was in their old people's home . . .'

'Oh. My God. I might know a few things about that. But go on, yeah?'

'. . . and it's a bit painful, but I think she may have . . . I worry that there might have been . . .'

'I think I know what you are about to say.'

'What?'

'No, you go first. What were you going to say?'

'Well, this Stern bloke. He revoked his will and left everything to her.'

'Ah. You know about that. OK. But I don't know the name of the bloke, I just knew that it was going on at the time, I think you'd just been born, I don't know how old you were . . .'

'Could it have been 1965?'

'Quite possibly.'

'Right. Look at this.'

I held the two bits of photocopied paper – Jack Stern's will – up in the air.

'Let me see.'

She studied them for twenty seconds.

'Oh my God . . . are you here in a legal capacity, as a lawyer?'

'No! I'm writing a book, about all the things she got up to. All the funny, entertaining stuff. I'm telling all the funny stories . . .'

'Yeah, but there are some not-so-funny stories . . .'

'Well, that's why I'm here. And it's hard to do a book like this, to come across this Stern business, and leave it out. He was eighty-three, he revoked his will, and he left it all to her. He left everything to her. I need to know why. And actually . . . more importantly . . . how.'

Silence.

'But did you not have any inkling of this before? Has it come as a big shock to you?'

'I knew fuck-all about it. No one told me. You didn't, did you? It only came up when Maurice sent me an e-mail, mentioning Stern's name. And I only started sniffing around because there was this journalist, this old hack, one day, and he started looking at me in a funny way and going, "Maitland, Maitland, I know that name." But look: we don't know anything for sure yet. He may have left her everything because he wanted to.'

'Have you spoken to Dad about this?'

'No, not yet. Do you think I need to?'

'Just a bit. I mean, Dad would have been happy to have just had a nice family life, a normal time, run the business and do it on the level. But she was always pushing the boundaries . . . she was always reaching out, pushing for more to try and prove her power.'

'God, it sounds like Macbeth and Lady Macbeth.'

'Yes that's just how it was.'

'Right . . . So what do you make of this, then?' I said, waving the photocopies in the air once more. 'Doesn't look good on the surface, does it?'

'No. Well, look. Let me tell you what I know.'

Here it comes. I get the feeling I am about to take a giant stride into the unknown. Rachel is cupping her mug of tea in her hands and steadying herself.

'I can remember at the time that there was a lot of secrecy and subterfuge going on. They used to have these little arguments, softly spoken little arguments, and he'd be arguing with her, trying to talk her out of things. And I never realized exactly what it was. But there was one argument I really remember like it was yesterday. I was quite bright at that time, I was only twelve or thirteen, but I picked up on things . . . and one day I heard them arguing about a will. I can't remember whose it was. And I remember saying to Mum, 'Why are you arguing about a will, Mum?'

Rachel wasn't looking at me at this stage. She was staring into space, tugging at memories. Her voice became slower and more deliberate . . .

'And I remember . . . her . . . getting Dad . . . to make this old man . . . sign . . . a will . . . in their favour. That's what I remember.'

Late January 1987

It was Pete, I think, who rang me up and told me that she'd been taken into hospital. St Helier hospital in Sutton: where he'd been born. He said she'd turned yellow and that maybe I should go and visit her. Neither of us said anything about it being serious or not: it just seemed like another turn of the wheel. I was coming up to London that weekend, I said, so I'd pop in and see her then.

St Helier hospital is one of the most depressing places on this earth. It's old, dirty and in a horribly run-down area of Sutton. My mother was on a floor that reeked of boiled cabbage, piss and bandages. It reminded me of boarding school and prison. She had her own room. She was indeed yellow. A dirty, slightly bruised yellow. She showed no emotion when she saw me. She was very tired. There was no light in her eyes. We talked about the future.

'I am going to sell Egmont Road,' she said, quietly.

'Why?'

'Because I cannot run it properly any more. I will go into a home. I will go into a home, they can look after me there. It will be all right. Why are you crying?'

'I don't know. I just am. I think I have seen somewhere in Bristol I want to buy. It's a flat.'

'Don't buy a flat. Buy a house. Never buy a flat.'

'Why? This one's really nice.'

'No. Always buy a house. Then you can rent it out. If you buy a flat I won't help you with the deposit. If you buy a house, I buy it for you.'

She knew I always had difficulty disobeying her. Especially when there was money on offer. She had a bit of a hold over me that way. She was growing more and more tired. There would be plenty more opportunities to talk about it later, I thought. I kissed her and left her on her own. I would see her again in the next couple of weeks, I said.

13 August 2005,
10.42 a.m.–11.33 a.m.

'How do you know that's what it was?' I said. 'How do you know that's what happened? Were you there when it happened?'

'Not when it happened, but I was outside, I was around.'

'What do you mean? Outside the room?'

'Yeah! I mean, it was just after school, I think. 357 London Road, Ewell.'

'Did you see them signing the will?'

'No I didn't . . . but I was definitely a curious child and I wanted to know what was going on.'

She went into stream-of-consciousness mode, like someone undergoing regression therapy. 'I remember saying, "What's going on?" And I remember her saying, "Get him to sign it, Irving, get him to sign it." "No. You can't do that, Bru. You can't." That's what he said.'

'Oh my God. That's pretty chilling.'

We sat in silence.

'So this would have been when?' I asked. 'Mid-sixties?'

'Yes, that's right, around then.'

'1965, like I said?'

'Why 1965?'

'Because that's when Stern changed his will and left everything to our mother.

Look at the date. Here.'

I pointed to the bit of the document that said 'this 24th day of October one thousand nine hundred and sixty-five'.

More silence.

'I'm as certain as I can be that this is what they were going on about. The date, the place, everything, it all fits. Like I said, I would have been twelve or thirteen at the time.'

'In which case I am as sure as I can be that something pretty terrible went on.'

'Here you are, on television, hunting down criminals, and your own mother was a criminal.'

'Well, we don't know that for sure, yet. Although the irony isn't lost on me. If this was happening today, I'd be doing a programme on her.'

Rachel started laughing, cackling. The exact same laugh as my mother's.

'There's another irony, you know,' she went on. 'She used to accuse all sorts of people of all sorts of crimes, including me! But most of them, all of them, were completely unfounded.'

'But with this Stern stuff . . . did she not realize that what she was doing was wrong?'

'Yes.'

'How do you know?'

'Because that's the way she was. She used to love to push the boundaries and I think she just lost sight of what was right and wrong.'

'And did you say to her, "Mum, why did you get that man to sign. . ."'?

'No. Because I was only twelve or thirteen at the time. But I did ask Dad what was going on and he said, 'It's all right darling, it's something about a will.''

We were left to our own thoughts once more. There was no emotion yet: it was too early for that. The enormity of what Rachel had revealed – apparently revealed, I should say – hadn't begun to register. Right now it felt as if we were discussing an incident that had nothing to do with us, not something that involved our own parents. Rachel spoke first. She said exactly what I had been thinking.

'I wonder if it happened more than once? 'Cos that's what criminals do, isn't it? They reoffend.'

'Stop calling her a criminal. I dunno about any others. I'd rather not go there just yet. I'll tell you what's worrying about this, though – he looks like the perfect victim. Old, no close relatives, no one to keep an eye on him . . . and loads of money.'

'It does look that way, doesn't it? They picked him. Or she did.'

'But . . . just because you do something wicked, it doesn't make you a wicked person, does it? It just means that you've done something wicked. She was capable of great acts of generosity and kindness . . . you know that.'

'Does it make you feel better to think that?'

'Well, like I say, I am just trying to justify it. And I think I feel a bit ashamed.'

'Why should you feel ashamed?'

'Because as someone said, the sins of the parents are visited on the children, aren't they?'

'Not necessarily. You're being superstitious. I mean, what about these terrible murdering sons of bitches, they murder and rape and God knows what, and the mothers, they're as sweet as pie . . . they've never done anything wrong, they've brought their sons up in the best possible way. Does that make the mothers murderers?'

'No. True.'

'Now let's see.' She picked up the copy of the will again and started studying it. 'God . . . where did you get this from?'

'Probate House in London. They keep all the wills there.'

'It's really surreal.'

'It's a smoking gun, that's what it is. Or at least one part of one. The trigger maybe.'

She carried on reading. When she came to the name of the executor of the will she smiled.

'Humphrey Benson! Do you remember him?'

'Yes I do. He lives in France now.'

'Lovely man. There was a funny story, you know. Not really related to this. Well, actually, maybe it is. Let me tell it to you quickly, you seem like you're in a hurry.'

'It's OK, we've got plenty of time.'

'Well, I had this accident. D'you remember? I fell off a bus. Complete accident.'

'No. Actually . . . maybe.'

'Well, I did, anyway. And I was in hospital, recuperating. And I knew she was coming, and she turned up with Dad and Humphrey. And he was very nice, and he said, "Look, we're not going to force you into doing anything you don't want to do," and I was looking at Dad, 'cos I was just fourteen, you know, I was just a child. And Humphrey said, "Your mother wants to sue the bus company".'

'Ah, yes . . . that old tactic. Not a crime, necessarily.'

'Yes, but it wasn't the bus company's fault. And I knew, I could sense, she wanted to manipulate me into saying it was the bus company's fault, or whatever. But Humphrey was very patient and kind and he said, "Tell me what happened." So I said, "Well, I just jumped off, and I got it wrong, it was going too fast." And she looked really disappointed. And she didn't talk to me for a while after that.'

'He doesn't remember anything about this, unfortunately,' I said, pointing to the will.

'Well, he wouldn't have known about it, would he? You don't tell your solicitor that you're up to no good, do you?'

'No, I suppose you don't. But he might have guessed there was something iffy about it, later on. Maurice says he saw a letter from Humphrey's lot, about a bloke called Stern, and a will, years ago. This must have been what it was about. It's all starting to make sense.'

'Did she get the money in the end? From this will?'

'I'm not sure. I don't think so . . . I guess that's what the letter was about. It would be great to see it but God knows how we get hold of it. It must be long gone.'

'He was a good solicitor. Sorry for drawing parallels here but what about . . . who was it, that bloke, the one who knocked off his patients?'

'There were quite a few.'

'Well, whichever one it was . . . this was how he was found out, right? He'd killed all of those people, nobody had twigged, and one of the daughters who was a solicitor looked at the will and said, "Hold on, why is the doctor getting everything? I'm the next in line."'

'Bit of an extreme parallel.'

'Yes, it's horrible to think like that. But it does make you think, doesn't it?'

'Oh, for God's sake.'

'Well, there were lots of elderly people, just dumped there by relatives. You have to think about it. You must keep an open mind.'

'Whose side are you on?'

'Whose side are *you* on?'

'I don't know. The truth, I guess. But that sounds a bit wanky. I'm not even sure what I'm getting into here, to be honest. But look. It's one thing to get someone to sign a will when you shouldn't but quite another to do what you're suggesting. And it is our mother we're talking about here . . . I just wonder, though, if this is why the old people's homes were closed down.'

'I don't know. All I remember at the time was her saying that it was just too much like hard work. But I guess she would say that.'

Rachel looked at the will again. She had been fiddling with it, nervously, but now she was studying the detail. She looked at page 2 and the bit where the value of the estate had been typed in. She read aloud.

'. . . the net value of the estate amounts to eighteen thousand three hundred and ninety pounds . . .'

She looked up.

'How much is that nowadays?'

'I'm not sure. Put it this way – if you'd bought a house with it then, that house would be worth half a million now. Maybe more. A million even.'

'Oh my God,' said Rachel. 'That's incredible. Who signed this, though? I mean, who witnessed it?'

'It's there, on the front page, look . . . a couple of old boys who were at Twin Gables at the time. Here we are . . . there're their signatures. Mr Robertson and Mr Wright. According to the law they would have needed to be present, in the room, I mean, at the very moment Stern signed, but God knows if they were.

Knowing her she probably gave them a bottle of champagne or something to keep them sweet. It's a shame you weren't there when he signed.'

'Well, I would have remembered if I had been, wouldn't I? But I was around that day. And I know which room it was in.'

'Oh yeah? I always imagined it, in my mind's eye, taking place in that room next to the bar.'

'No.'

She started drawing a diagram on the back of the will, in pencil.

'You remember that extension they built, to the side? It was in that room. The one on the first floor, to the right, as you look at the front.'

'Oh God, yeah. I can see it now. I know exactly which one you mean. You remember rooms, don't you? I remember the one where she pretended to die in front of me.'

'Well, to be honest I've felt really guilty over the years because I didn't believe her when she said she had cancer.'

'Join the club. It was like the woman who cried wolf. You can hardly blame us.'

'Yes, but it was true, she did have cancer. But to be honest I didn't take as much interest as I should have done because she seemed so strong and such a survivor that I thought, well, whatever she has got, she'll be OK anyway.'

'I know exactly what you mean. But I would just like to know when it was true. Like, when did it start becoming truer than it had been? I mean, not that it matters now, but I'm fairly sure she didn't have cancer of the eyebrows.'

'What?'

I explained the story to her. We laughed. We were getting on. It wasn't nearly as awkward or difficult as I had thought it would be.

'I must say, it's lovely to see you. I haven't spoken to my daughter Joanne for years but then when she heard about my illness she came back to me . . . that's her on the wall with her daughter and her husband, he's a lovely, lovely man, he's an architect, you know . . . and now you're here so that's wonderful too.'

'And how is your illness?'

'Well, I have cancer of the ovaries but it's in remission. They have taken out everything that they can take out of me so hopefully it'll be OK.'

I should have been more sympathetic to her but she seemed so nonchalant about it that I let it pass.

'Why?' I said. 'Why? Why did she do it?'

'She was a control freak.'

'Oh God, don't give me that. That's everyone's pat, cod psychological explanation for everything. This is more than being a control freak. Actually . . . maybe we've got the wrong end of the stick. Maybe he said, "Yup, they've done me a great job, I wanna leave everything to them." I mean, are you sure you're not imagining all this stuff, this 'get him to sign" business?'

'Look. Let me tell you. I am in no doubt. I have total faith in my own judgement. Because I have been told by lots of people, and I know this to be true anyway, that I am very good on detail . . .'

'Like Pete, you mean,' I interrupted. 'As in remembering scraps of conversations, verbatim, from years ago.'

'Exactly! Family trait. I don't miss anything. And I stick it here . . .'

She pointed to her head. '. . . and I absorb it and I stick it in my computer and when it comes up, I . . .'

'OK. Is there *any* positive gloss you can put on that? On what happened, on what you heard?'

'No. There is nothing I can tell you that I would have misunderstood, that I would have misheard.'

'But it was forty years ago . . . but then I suppose, if you remember it, you remember it.'

'Of course I do. And I'll tell you why I remember it. Because, you know, dads and daughters are usually very close. There's a bond there. Dads are usually very protective towards their daughters. And it was the case with us and so whenever I saw Dad upset I would get very protective and go to his aid. And I saw that he was upset, I can see it in my mind's eye now that he was very emotional, on the verge of tears. I remember distinctly, can't you see it in my face, I'm seeing it, I'm living it now, I remember, they were arguing, and I was saying what's the matter, Dad, then they would go off again and argue a bit more, it was all to do with that room, that room that the old boy was in. They would come in and out, in and out.'

'Hmm.'

'And Mum was adamant. "No, you must get him to sign, you must get him to sign." And then there was a kerfuffle, and something about "the will, the will", and also, I cared about those old people, you know . . . I used to care about what happened to them. I used to look after them when I came home from school.'

'Why didn't he stop her? He . . . he was weak, wasn't he?'

'Yes. But he loved her. He loved her very much. I know it was wrong, what he did . . .' She corrected herself. 'What *they* did, what she got him to do. But if he didn't do what she wanted, then the marriage would have disintegrated.'

'How do you know?'

'That's how it was between them. She was forever saying "Do this, or else". She would tell him what to do and he did it . . . because he wanted a quiet life. And because he loved her. They had a good business, they'd built it up, they had prestige. And he didn't want to lose all that.'

'Hmm. Possibly.'

'Me personally, though, if it had been me, and my partner was up to no good, I would have said, "Look, stop this now, or I am leaving you." Wouldn't you?'

'I like to think so. What is it they say? "For evil to flourish, it is only necessary for good men to do nothing."'

'Exactly.'

'God. What a choice. He was weighing up, on the one hand, do I do this . . . this terrible thing . . . but on the other, if I don't, I lose my family. And the irony is, he went ahead and did it and lost his family anyway.'

'It's tragic. That's what it is. But she was ruthless, our mother, ruthless.'

'Why do I keep coming back to Macbeth and Lady Macbeth?'

'Because that's what it was.'

'Well, I can always ask him, I suppose.'

'Ask him what?'

'Why. Why did you do it? Or let it happen? And how?'

'How will you do that? On the phone?'

'No . . . I've written to him. I'm going out there in two weeks.'

'Well, don't be too hard on him.'

'Of course I won't . . . he's my dad and he's in his eighties, for Christ's sake. There are questions to be asked, clearly. But I mean, of course I'll be gentle. It may be that he wants to talk about it, you never know. I mean, I'm not going over there to point the finger, I'm just going over there to say, "Come on, spill. Tell me everything."'

'But be careful how you put it . . . say, "How do you feel about it all?" Not "Do you feel bad?" Just ask him how he was feeling, what he was thinking.'

'Rearrange the following words into a well-known phrase or saying. Grannies. Eggs. Suck. Don't. Teach.'

'What?'

'Don't teach your granny how to suck eggs. I am an interviewer, you know . . . I do it for a living.'

'Yes, but this is different. It's not an interview. He's your father, not some conman you're confronting on the street.'

'Yeah, I know, I know. Look . . . I'll just let it happen naturally. It's bound to just . . . come out.'

She looked lost. She was gazing in the general direction of the freezer but she certainly wasn't thinking about its contents.

'He probably couldn't sleep at night . . . probably still can't, poor thing.'

'On balance I feel slightly more sorry for Mr Stern. I mean, they were lucky one of them didn't get put in the slammer. Our lives would have been different then, wouldn't they? We wouldn't be here now, for a start. I wouldn't have my job, the one I've got now, would I? I'd have been taken out of school . . . God knows what would have happened. God, it could have been so different. Thank fuck they didn't get found out . . . or maybe they did. Maybe there was a deal? I dunno.'

'Well, do we know if they took the money?'

'Crucial question. I have no idea. Dad wouldn't have seen any of it, though, as they had got divorced by the time it came through. So she would have copped the lot. I'm going to have a pop at Humphrey Benson and see if he can remember . . . but the omens aren't good.'

'What do you mean?'

'He told me he couldn't remember anything about anything, basically. So he's unlikely to remember individual pieces of paper like paying-in slips, is he?'

'No. Actually, I've got some pieces of paper. When I knew you were coming, I made some notes about things. I was going to write a book once, you see, but I gave up in the end.'

She leant over and took a scrap of paper off the sideboard. I recognized the handwriting on it even though I hadn't seen it in two decades. Large, wild Biro-nic scrawls.

'Um . . . I've just written bits and pieces,' she said, fiddling nervously with her crib sheet.

'Ask me what you want.'

'Nursing homes . . . overcrowding . . . charging the same rate for a single as a double . . .'

'Oh yes? What was that?'

'They'd charge the same rate for a room . . .'

'No, not that. The overcrowding thing.'

'There were limits on how many old people you could have in a home, I think. I mean, they weren't stuffing them in ten to a room, or anything like that . . .'

'Like at 20 Egmont Road, you mean.'

'Ha ha ha ha! Yes! No, it wasn't like that. She owned other houses in London Road, do you remember?'

'Of course . . . I stayed in them! 335 London Road, Ewell. And 361. And . . . we even owned 351, didn't we? Monopoly'

'Yes, well, the thing is, they only had permission from the council to have old people in the main home, you know, 355 and 357. But they used to put old people in their other houses anyway, when they were full up in the main home. But the council smelt a rat, I think. And they used to come calling, to inspect all the properties, to see what was going on. And I used to have to take the old people out into the garden and hide them! I mean, sometimes it was a carer or a nurse who would do it. Can you imagine, me a fourteen-year-old girl, hiding in the bushes with an old person? But I did! I remember, even as a teenager, thinking, "This is weird!" and I remember there was a lovely old man, it might even have been Stern, actually, he was paralysed, I used to have to feed him, clothe him, everything, and one day I had to take him to the bottom of the garden and hide him behind a tree and stay there for half an hour while the council were looking round for evidence.'

After what we had been talking about the image of hiding an old buffer behind a tree came as a bit of light relief. It's not every day you get to hide small, crusty old men behind the rhododendron in your back garden.

'Quite funny, isn't it?' I said.

'What?'

'Hiding an old man behind a tree.'

'Do you know . . . he didn't even care. I'm not sure he even knew what was going on.'

Her dogs started yelping. All three at once. They invaded the kitchen, turning it into a canine disco. 'All right, darlings,' she cooed, bending down to try to mollify them while simultaneously looking at the notes she'd written.

'Oh, by the way, you know I've changed my name now?'

'Really? What is it?'

'Maitland. I've changed it officially.'

'I thought it was Coutts.' She had taken the name about ten years ago, I had heard on the grapevine, in the hope that some of the bank's cachet would rub off on her. Before that she was known as Chequer – her married name. Before that she was Rachel Melman. There were a few others on the way, as well. She and my mother must have been very popular with the deed poll people.

'Right, OK . . . boarding school . . . no, that's about you, that's got nothing to do with it . . . the hotel . . . that's something else . . . when they changed over, the gay thing . . .'

'Oh yes, I know all that.I got all the cuttings from the newspaper.'

'I remember how upset you were. At school you used to say, "Oh God, I can't face it, they'll tease me." Poor thing.'

'Was it that bad? I don't remember it being that bad.' I really don't remember it being that bad. Maybe my memory pilot pressed the ejector button, I don't know.

'Anyway, those are my notes.'

'I think I am going to have to go and lie in a darkened room now.'

'Listen . . . if there's anything else you want to know . . .'

'I know too much already.'

'I'm sorry, Jonny, but you asked me.'

We walked out of the house. I got in my car and wound the window down.

'We should talk again.'

'Yes, but look, you can't not see someone for twenty years as we have and just . . . give me a bit of time . . .'

'I'm not expecting to see you every week, Jonny, don't worry.'

'OK, look, you can meet my wife, maybe . . . at the end of the summer.'

'Lovely. I've seen the pictures. She looks very nice. Look, I don't mind if you don't want to talk to me ever again, I don't mind.'

'No no no, it's just that . . .'

'Whichever way you want to play it, I'm fine. As Dad would say, better late than never.'

'It's very difficult, with families. You don't have the same relationship with your family that you do with your friends.'

'Yes, but whatever happens I've seen you now. I feel reborn.'

'Right. Er . . . cheers.'

11 February 1987

The second time I visited my mother in St Helier hospital we didn't have a conversation. We couldn't. She was incapable of saying anything. She didn't, as far as I could tell, even recognize me or know what was going on. She was lying on her side, in bed, and although there were sounds emanating from her, they were not recognizable. She was babbling: a strange stream of noise was coming out of her mouth. Tics, tuts, breaths, blows and, occasionally, something that sounded as if it might be a word. Her face was pale, sickly yellow, but her brown eyes were ablaze with fear. They talked, even if she could not. She was utterly petrified, bewildered. I sat there, on my own, looking at her. I didn't feel distress. She couldn't be dying. She had been ill before – although perhaps not as ill as she sometimes made out – and made a recovery. And she would recover this time, too. Of that there was no doubt.

15 August 2005

Last night I dreamt that I was a contestant on *Mastermind* and that my specialist subject was the history of the Stern family. I scored fourteen points and no passes but my general knowledge let me down and I came second. It went something like this:

JOHN HUMPHRYS: 'When was the famous Stern and Parsons Countrywide Estate Agency firm founded?'

ME: '1882.'

JOHN HUMPHRYS: 'Correct. Which Stern married Amelie Devereux in 1892?'

ME: 'Sir Edward Jolliffe Stern.'

JOHN HUMPHRYS: 'Correct.'

And so on.

The dream was still wafting around my brain when I called what felt like my fifty-fourth Stern this year. This time it was Jean Stern. She, like my last two Sterns, was in her eighties.

She let me know, very early on in the conversation, 'just to put you in the picture', that she was the mother of someone called

Lord Waverleigh. She was also, we eventually established, a distant relative of Jack Stern. And I mean distant. As in Land's End
to John o' Groats: Jack Stern was her father-in-law's cousin. Got
that? I was on the phone to the cousin by marriage, once
removed, of the man at the centre of my enquiries. Even so, she
knew him, all right. She was also very posh indeed. She sounded
like a lady-in-waiting to the Queen. I went over the story with
her. Curiously, as with all the other Sterns I've spoken to, Jean
expressed no great shock or disapproval when I got to the central allegation. Just a mildly startled 'Ew . . . really?' Strange: this
is her family's money we're talking about here, after all. Albeit
heavily extended family money. Jean was my big hope: she had,
after all, been described by another Stern as the family historian.
But she wasn't, it turned out. That honour went to someone else.
Yes . . . another Stern.

'I have got my cousin living with me here. Guy Stern. He
might know if there was a scandal about Uncle Jack's will. He's
had a stroke, but it hasn't affected his brain at all. I can talk to
him. What did you say your name was again?'

I didn't want to lose her that quickly. Did she remember Jack
Stern?

'Uncle Jack? Oh yes. We all called him Jack. He was always a
little bit funny. He married a rich person . . . Dewar was her
name. She came from a very well-to-do family. So the children,
Jack's children, Edward and Joan, were quite comfortably orff.'

'Ah yes . . . Joan went into a home, didn't she, she's been there
for fifty years, I've been told.'

'Goodness me, you have been doing your homework. Yes, she
was quite extraordinary. But she can't help you now, I'm afraid. It
really is most annoying, as most of the people who would know
what happened with this story have died. But Guy Stern might
know. His brain is OK. I could certainly ask him about Maitland.'

'Well, please do. There must have been a bit of a hoo-hah. I'm sure he would remember.'

'Do you think there was a hoo-hah?'

'Well, now you come to mention it I'm beginning to have a horrible feeling in the pit of my stomach that maybe there wasn't. And that even though my mother's solicitors may have warned her not to take the money, she just took it, anyway.'

'Well, the only thing we can say is that Joan, his daughter, had plenty of money and no children and Edward, her brother, was very rich and he also had no children. He lived in a very big house, you see. But he is gone now.'

'But presumably he would have made a fuss about it if he thought someone was making off with his birthright?'

'Lord, no. He wasn't the type to do that. He wouldn't have cared. He had lots of the stuff. So you see, they didn't need any money . . . so if your mother got it . . .'

She seemed to be shaping up to say that if my mother had indeed got the money, it didn't really matter.

'Well, that's an interesting way of looking at it. But I'm just trying to establish if anyone complained or smelt a rat . . . I mean, Jack's wife . . . I've got your family tree here, I'm just looking at it now, Jack's wife, she was . . . let's see . . . she died in 1919, which is fifty years before him. So she wouldn't have made a fuss either, obviously, 'cos she'd been dead for fifty years. And she had a brother, but he died in 1947. So Jack had no close relatives . . . if anyone was going to kick off, it would have been Jack's son, I guess. What was he like?'

'Lovely man. Charming,'

'What . . . too charming to make a fuss, that sort?'

'Quite. What I can say to you, though, is that those two children of Jack's, they were well orff. And I don't think Jack himself had a lot of money anyway.'

'Well, he left twenty thousand pounds . . .'

'Well, that's not very much.'

'It was in those days. If you spent twenty grand on a house in 1969 it could be worth half a million now, even more.'

'Ye-es. He was clever, you know. He used to be clever.'

'What did he do?'

'Well, he was a bit dotty, you know, a bit schitzy. I think he was in business with his father a bit, when he was young. His father was the chief agriculturalist in the country.'

We left it there. I asked her to phone me if her cousin, the one who had had the stroke, remembered anything fishy or controversial. He, we agreed, was the last throw of the dice on this one.

Then I called Humphrey Benson again. I figured he'd be wanting an update. And who knows? Maybe my discoveries might jog his memory. I had been a bit frustrated, to be honest, that he couldn't remember anything about this case. How could he not? It wasn't that I didn't believe him when he said he couldn't remember, of course. But surely, if you were a lawyer, something like this would stick in your mind. But then again he is in his seventies now and this was a very long time ago. And what seems hugely important to me now would have been merely run-of-the-mill to him, back then. He would have dealt with literally thousands of cases in his lifetime, some of them far more remarkable and extraordinary than this. My mother may have been 'his most amazing client' but that doesn't necessarily mean that he should now have perfect recall, forty-odd years on, of every detail of every case he handled for her.

I read the will to him over the phone and reminded him that he was one of the executors. They are the people – usually it's a lawyer and/or a trusted friend of the deceased – who are entrusted by the courts with the authority to hand out the money. There were two executors in this case: the other was a bloke called Bruce Carter, Humphrey's partner in Benson and Co. I told Humphrey that all roads pointed very much to the fact that Mr Stern had been coerced into signing the will.

'Who witnessed the signing?' he asked me.

'Two old geezers who were living in Twin Gables at the time. Allegedly.'

'Ah. Right.'

'I'm just trying to establish whether she took the money, that's all.'

'Yes, well, I spoke to Nicholas Carstairs about this a few weeks ago . . .'

Nicholas Carstairs, you will recall, is the sports car restoration enthusiast who ran Humphrey's firm in the late sixties and seventies – it was he who put me in touch with Humphrey in the first place.

'. . . and I think he may be able to shed light on this letter your brother saw all those years ago.'

'That would be excellent.'

'Well, he seemed quite definite a week or two ago that I did write and say, "You really can't go on with this." In other words I, or we, whatever, would have advised your mother not to claim the inheritance left to her by this Stern character.'

'What would have made you do that?'

'I have no idea. I have no recollection of this very important incident at all. But Bruce Carter might know. Just let me explain, Jonathan. I would not have had anything to do with the administration of the estate. Because my partner Bruce Carter, who was my junior partner, was responsible for that sort of thing. So what I suggest you do, Jonathan, is to talk to Nicholas Carstairs and ask him what you should do next. I expect he will put you in touch with Bruce. You must talk to him.'

'Is he still alive?'

'Oh yes, he's younger than me. But you have made a very important step in the right direction. We know that the will was proved. All we need to do now is try and find out what happened to the money.'

'Quite. But it may not be that easy. My mother's finances were . . . labyrinthine, I think is the word.'

'Ha ha ha ha ha! Yes. Do let me know what happens, won't you?'

'Of course.'

Next stop, Nick Carstairs. When I first spoke to him he had been understandably cagey, what with me ringing up out of the blue and asking questions about things that happened half a lifetime ago. But following his recent chat with Humphrey, his memory had been well and truly jogged into shape. He was now much more helpful than he had been before – almost enthusiastic.

'Oh yes, I remember it very clearly now . . . not in detail, because I wasn't handling it. But obviously something like that, which was a quite . . . you know, a notorious situation, we used to discuss round the lunch table.'

'Why? Because there was a bit of a whiff about it?'

'No, it was more than that, it wasn't just instinct, it was . . . you know . . . legal convention . . . We have to go back a bit here and I'm speaking off the cuff, because it's fifty years since I did the exams, but with wills, there was always what they called 'a presumption of undue influence' between teacher and pupil, doctor and patient . . .'

'Oh yeah, that sounds familiar. Like, when one leaves money to the other, alarm bells start ringing?'

'Yes, absolutely.'

'So there would have been this 'presumption of undue influence' when, for example, an old geezer in an old people's home left everything he had to the owner.'

'Oh yes, absolutely. When one party is in a stronger position than the other, because of the dependency factor, that person is automatically assumed to have exerted undue influence.'

'And so in this case your alarm bells would have rung off the hook, so to speak.'

'Yes. But as against that, you might well get cases where the family, quite frankly, don't go near the old person and the old person says, "My family have deserted me, I want you to benefit."'

'I'm not sure this was one of those cases. I'm reasonably confident there was a fair bit of undue influence going on. I mean, I have a pretty dependable witness who has no reason to make it all up.'

'Oh yes? Who's that?'

'My sister. She was there at the time and heard my mother telling my father to get Mr Stern to sign.'

'Good grief.'

'I just want to know whether she took the money, though. My dad might know . . . I am going to talk to him about it, if I can. He's in America.'

'Well, you might like to ask your father by the way – and I say this with the utmost hesitation and deference – whether he can remember any other cases.'

'Yes, you're not the first person to have suggested that.'

'Because I just . . . I can't, I . . . don't want to, you know, I couldn't name a name, I may be doing your mother a grave injustice, but I . . . I know there was always . . . there were always, how shall I say, litigious-type problems on. Whether it was about overcharging or the other, you know, I don't know. But while she was with us, she was a very intensive client. There was always something on.'

'Yes, I bet. Good news for you guys . . . if not for her residents perhaps.'

'Well, yes. Quite.

'It's just a pity you can't remember the details – not that I'm blaming you or anything, it was the last century, after all.'

'Well, to be honest our memories are not what they were. I mean, it was quite obvious when I spoke to Humphrey that he couldn't remember. And it will be the same with Bruce. His memory is dreadful.We set up an office in Reading together and Bruce can hardly remember anything about it. But you must remember, we went through literally tens of thousands of clients together.'

'I know. I've been thinking about that. I should at least speak to Bruce, though.'

'Bruce is quite set in his ways and I would expect he might be a bit hesitant about all this. He might clam up, you just coming out of the blue like this. I mean, some things are best left in the mists of time, you know.'

'I know. I've been thinking about that too. But I want to carry on.'

'Yes, but what's the outcome going to be? Don't use the dreaded word "closure", will you?'

'Well . . . a book. To be honest, my investigative juices are running. More than that, though . . . I want to . . . know my parents, I guess. I thought I knew them. . .well, my mum, anyway . . . quite well. And it's beginning to dawn on me that maybe I didn't. Know her as well as I thought I did, at any rate. And I just really want to know what happened. And you know . . . it's just a great story, there is that . . . How do I get in touch with Bruce, by the way?'

'He's in the phone book.'

And so he was. He lived in Oxshott, a few miles from Epsom. A hat trick of septuagenarian lawyers. And all before dinner.

Reading, or rather hearing, between the lines of what his two

old work colleagues had told me, I was expecting Bruce Carter
to a be a little wary. But he was polite and helpful.

'Why, we were talking about your mother only the other day,'
he said, after I'd introduced myself but before I'd gone into any
details.

'How so?' I said, assuming it had something to do with the
matter in hand.

'We were just saying what a great woman she was, is . . . I
mean, we're not in touch with her any more, obviously, but she
was very good to us. She had a lovely Spanish girl working for
her, Lolita was her name, and she decided that she was too good
for her, you know, she was a very educated, classy girl and she
was just doing the washing up, basically, for your mother, so she
sent her to us and we gave her a job as a nanny and we are still
friends with her to this day. Yes, quite a character, your mother.'

It was good to hear something positive for a change. I
repeated the story yet again and yet again the lawyer at the other
end of the line could recall only the vaguest details. But there
was a chance, he said, that he might be able to shed some light
on the matter as he was due to go into the offices of Benson and
Co. quite soon. He still did stuff for them, he said, occasionally,
on a consultancy basis.

'Well, please do call,' I said, thanking him for helping me,
'whether you find out anything or not. I don't want to let this go
until I've explored all the avenues.'

17 August 2005

From: Mmaitland@xxxxxxxx
To: Jmaitland@xxxxxxx
Sent: August 17 2005, 13:21
Subject: Confession

I haven't told you this before. For various reasons. But when our mother went into hospital in 1987 I asked her about the Stern business. She turned away and said, 'He had too much money anyway.'

By the way, you also might be interested to know that Sid James, of 'Carry On Up the Castle/Khyber/Desert etc.' fame, wrote a letter of support to the local papers in the early sixties when local residents started complaining about the way the old people at Twin Gables were being treated.

Maurice

From: Jmaitland@xxxxxxx
To: Mmaitland@xxxxx
Sent: August 17 2005, 13:26
Subject: Re: Confession

That is extraordinary. What did you ask her? What else did you say? What else did she say? What was her attitude?

Jonny

From: Mmaitland@xxxxxx
To: Jmaitland@xxxxx
Sent: August 17 2005, 13:28
Subject: Re: re: Confession

My tone was inquisitive rather than inquisitorial. She was very ill, after all. But I was getting fed up with their evasiveness over this issue – I had periodically asked both of them about it over the years and never received a satisfactory response. When she said, 'He had enough money anyway,' that was, with hindsight, highly ambiguous. Looking back it is difficult to ascertain from that comment whether she accepted the inheritance or not. The way she clammed up and looked away made me think there was a whole lot more to the story – maybe the tip of an iceberg. Running into a proverbial brick wall, I did not try to draw her any more on the subject because of the state she was in, although she was compos mentis. I was really after a confession or an explanation: but I got neither.

Maurice

18 August 2005

I got a message on my mobile this morning, while I was in the car. I was on the way to Epsom to play cricket.

'Hello, Jonathan, it's Humphrey Benson here. I think we may be one step closer to getting the key to this problem. Nicholas Carstairs has very kindly done some detective work, you'll be pleased to hear, and he's actually located the ledger cards for your mother, for all the jobs we did for her. Some of it is really rather interesting. Why don't you give me a call. Cheerio.'

The moment I got back home I called France. It was dark outside and I was still in my cricket whites.

'Humphrey . . . it's Jonathan. I got your call. This is turning into an episode of *Poirot*.'

'It certainly is.'

Humphrey told me what had happened. Nicholas Carstairs found that his curiosity had been aroused by my phone call. So he decided to nip down to his old office at Benson and Co. and root around in the basement. The only records he could find relating to the sixties and seventies were things called ledger cards. These were small pieces of card on which were written the barest details about every single job Benson and Co. undertook:

the client's name and address, a reference number and a two-word description of what it was all about. Nicholas Carstairs then photocopied every single ledger card with the name 'Maitland' on it and sent then to Humphrey.

'So I've got it all in front of me now. There are massive amounts of cards, starting in April 1961, and I'm just looking at them . . . here we go . . . May 1962, Maitland. Re: dispute . . . June 1963, Maitland. Re: purchase agreement . . . January '64, Maitland. Re: planning permission . . . goodness me, they were very good clients . . . ah, here we go, here it is. February the second 1965. Re: Loan from Stern.'

'What's that about?'

'It's what it says. Loan, from Stern.'

'What? They borrowed money off him?'

'That's right. And it was more than once . . . let's just pass on . . . sorry, I've got a lot of stuff to go through here . . . aha! Here we are. June the sixth, 1966. Promissory note to Mr Stern.'

'Is that another loan?'

'I don't know. I would imagine so.'

'Does it say how much it was for?'

'No. We filled out these cards just to keep track of all the cases we were doing. The actual papers themselves would long since have been destroyed. But this is of some interest, is it not?'

'It certainly is.'

'Hello, here's another one. Re: loan from Miss Someone or other. Sorry, can't read the handwriting on that one. Those were the only two cases, I think. Now are you listening carefully?'

'Yes.'

'If there were any problems with the Stern will, that would have been recorded under the ledger cards for Stern, not Maitland. Do you follow me?'

'Yes, absolutely. Because if there had been any shenanigans

the bill would have been paid by him . . . or rather his executors, i.e. you, out of the proceeds of his estate.'

'Absolutely.'

'So we've got to ask Nicholas Carstairs very nicely if he would go back to the office and see what the cards say for Stern. If they say anything at all.' And what we are looking for is a ledger card that says something like "1969, Re: Stern will dispute".'

'Precisely.'

'Thank you, Humphrey.'

'Not at all. Keep me posted.'

I sat down at the kitchen table and took stock. It's not exactly ethical behaviour to borrow money from the old people in your care, is it? More importantly, though, I wanted to work out the implications of what I'd just heard. Once I'd got it straight in my mind, I felt my stomach tightening. Legally, when Stern died, his debtors – i.e. my mother – still owed him. The actual debts survived his death. But now he was dead, his debtors owed that money to his estate instead. In other words, they owed it to his beneficiaries. And he left his money to only one person, of course: my mother. So all the money she previously owed him, before his death, she now owed to herself. In effect, all her debts to him had been cancelled. The big unanswered – and perhaps unanswerable – question was this: how much had she borrowed? I had one clue, or at least a possible indication, to work on. Soon after I went to Probate House in London I went back and took out a copy of another Stern will. That belonging to Mr Stern's brother. His name, you probably won't recall, was Edward Jolliffe Stern. I thought it might come in handy at some stage. It had now.

I went out to my office at the bottom of the garden. It was now well past midnight but I wanted to check the figures. The document showed that Edward Jolliffe Stern left roughly £150,000 in his will. It went to his immediate family. Let's assume, not unreasonably, that the two brothers were equally wealthy. One, Edward Jolliffe, died leaving £150,000. The other, John James, left just £20,000. How much of his wealth had been whittled away by the two loans he'd made to my mother: £2,000?; £5,000?; £20,000?; £50,000; £100,000?

Then there was still the other riddle. Had she actually claimed the £20,000 Stern inheritance? It would seem she had been advised by her lawyers not to. It was their legal duty to warn her and it seems they fulfilled it. But did she ignore them? I suspect so. Let's face it: if she was capable of 'inducing' an old man in her care to sign his entire estate over to her, she wouldn't have had too much of a problem ignoring the non-legally binding advice of a couple of solicitors from Epsom. I could check her bank accounts from that period, I suppose, to see if the Stern money was paid in, but that would be like searching for a fish at the bottom of a very busy ocean. It would be technically possible to find what I was looking for, if I was lucky. But there's every chance I would fail. My mother, you see, had several different accounts at several different banks. Some of the banks she had accounts with, in the sixties, don't even exist any more. I could spend a year, on a trial-and-error basis, asking every bank that ever existed in the Epsom and Ewell area to check their records to see whether they had a customer called Mrs Maitland. It's possible they might: some banks keep account details on microfilm, going as far back as fifty years. But even if I struck pay dirt and got her accounts from the relevant period – i.e. late 1969, when the money from the Stern will would have been paid in – that might not help. The relevant sum – £18,390 and 17 shillings – might not show up. It may have been disguised by splitting it up into smaller sums. Or it may have been paid in at a later date. And anyway: now that I know that she borrowed money off him and didn't have to pay it back, the question of whether she claimed the inheritance or not has become almost academic.

Even so, I wanted to dot the 'i's and cross the 't's and find out as much as I could about what happened. So I called Nicholas Carstairs. He seemed surprised to hear from me again but like his fellow retired lawyers was unfailingly polite and helpful. And his lawyer's mind was clearly still working well. He remembered telling me, in our last conversation, that Benson and Co. had no papers left relating to this period. But now he'd come up with these ledger cards. He wanted to explain the apparent discrepancy. He was being accurate when he told me there were no papers left, he said. Because these were cards, and an index system, not papers. It's OK, Nick, I told him, you don't have to cover yourself. I'm grateful that you're helping me at all. Yes, he said, he would look in the index system under 'Stern'. But for various reasons – client confidentiality, I guess – he didn't want to communicate the results of his search to me, but to Humphrey.

There was one other important thing to discuss. What did Mr Stern's will look like? he wanted to know. Was there a front page saying 'Prepared by Benson and Co.'?

No, I told him, there wasn't. Why was that significant?

'Because that means it was a homemade job. If we, our company, Bruce and Humphrey that is, had prepared the will, they would have gone to see Mr Stern and that would have meant finding out exactly what was going on. And they would have smelled a rat, no doubt. But this looks very much like a DIY job. If there is no title page, saying 'Benson and Co.', that means we didn't prepare it.'

'What . . . so you mean they would have knocked up the will on a typewriter, at home, or using a legal textbook and then presented it to Stern as a fait accompli?'

'Something like that.'

'Well, I must say I think the will was typewritten. I mean, it is . . . I'm looking at it now.'

'Interesting. There we go.'

'And she would have made your lot the executors, in your absence.'

'Quite. You can do that, you know.'

'And the first time you lot would have started taking any notice of the will, presumably, was when Stern died. Which is when you would have found out the contents of his will. And you then carried out your legal duty to the letter, by warning her not to accept the money.'

'You've got it.'

'Quite clever, really.'

I told him how grateful I was – three times – and said I would be dropping off a bottle of something soon. Did he like champagne?

'Good God, please, I don't want anything like that,' he said. 'No no no. No, please don't give me anything, there's no need to do that.'

19 August 2005

From: Jmaitland@xxxx
To: Mmaitland@xxxx
Sent: August 19 2005 12:56
Subject: Giant strides

Hi there

Are you ready for this? It appears our mother 'borrowed' money off Stern, at least twice, before his death. We don't know how much but it was probably a lot. Because she was his sole beneficiary, those debts were of course erased on his death. We still don't know for sure whether she claimed the inheritance, but as a betting man I know what my money is on. It also appears the will was a homemade job, i.e. knocked up by using legal textbooks. It gets worse.

Jonny

From: Mmaitland@xxxx
To: Jmaitland@xxxxxt
Sent: August 19 2005 14:12
Subject: Re: Giant Strides

Crikey! Reminds me of an old law case I studied where a lifetime
debt was wiped out by the debtor changing colours to become the
executor or beneficiary. No doubt your mother would have used the
school-fees argument to justify both of the loans. Interestingly, re:
the homemade will . . . there was a dog-eared and heavily
marked copy of *Everyman's Own Lawyer* in the family library in the
1960s, the inheritance chapter and specimens of which could well
have been the template for the Stern will. You are doing a great
job. I've been trying to get to the bottom of this saga myself for
many years but, being out of the country, can't do much.

Maurice

From: Jmaitland@xxxxx
To: Mmaitland@xxxxx
Sent: August 19 2005 15:51
Subject: Re: re: Giant strides

Thanks for that. I note with interest, as they say, the use of the
word 'your', as opposed to 'our', in the third line of your email. As
for your comments about the will: very interesting, too. I knew my –
our – law degrees would come in useful one day. One question
though. If you've been trying to get to the bottom of this saga for
many years, why didn't you tell me anything about it?

J

From: Mmaitland@xxxx
To: Jmaitland@xxxxx
Sent: August 19 2005 16:12
Subject: Re: re: re: Giant Strides

Why not tell you before? If I had started with just the skeletons in the family closet I knew about – far from a complete picture, given what is coming out now – your faith in both of our parents would have been shattered.

Maurice

PS: re: 'your' as opposed to 'our' . . . it was deliberate: but don't read too much into it.

20 August 2005

The tickets for my trip to America have come through. But there is someone else I need to see before I go. Someone who seemed to know more than she was willing to tell, when I started out on this journey. Now that I know what I know perhaps she will be more forthcoming. I am going to see her tomorrow.

21 August 2005

I hadn't told my Auntie Ruthie what my visit was about. But she cottoned on pretty quick. She asked me how I was.

'Not brilliant.'

'Why, my darling? Here, come and sit down, I have made breakfast for us.'

'Well . . . you were hinting at stuff when I came to see you last year and I've been doing a lot of finding out. Tell me if you knew about that.'

I handed her a copy of the Stern will and explained who he was. She read the front page and looked up at me. There was no surprise in her expression. Only resignation.

She said nothing for thirty seconds.

'Sadly . . . I knew that they were doing that.'

'Doing what?'

'Signing old people . . .'

'More than one?'

'More than one.'

'How do you know?'

'Directly from them. Because they bragged about it, Jonny. They didn't see anything wrong with it. Pretty ugly.'

'They bragged about it?'

'They bragged about it.'

'How many? A handful?'

'More than one, but I can't tell you how many, and I can't tell you specifically who.' She brandished the will. 'But you have put a name to it, here, and I don't know how you fished this out.'

'It wasn't that hard. I do it for a living.'

'There is worse, I am afraid. She very nearly . . .'

'What?'

'There was this old lady. And they managed to get her to sign her fortune over to them. All her wealth. And the family, the old lady's family, raised hell. And your parents took the old lady from Twin Gables and put her in their own house, on the top floor, in that big house in Dorking that they owned. And of course then they could charge her extortionate prices, because they could justify it to the relatives by saying, 'Look, she is living in this big house in Dorking, with us, in our home.' And of course the family kicked up even more of a fuss. And Bru couldn't stand it. She wanted the whole thing to end. She wanted the old lady to die, so she could inherit. So they actually discussed . . . methods.'

'How do you know that?'

'My mother was visiting from Israel . . . she was staying with them at the time. I wouldn't have known about this, if not for my mother . . . she was getting more and more nervous. And she rang me up and she said, "Ruthie, what shall I do?" And I said, "Look! Tell her! Tell her it will be their end! That if she thinks they are going to benefit from anything like that, no way. They are going to be found out." And she just went and sat with Bru and said, "For God's sake, just give them back the money. Do anything, but just get out of it. You will never win." But she was literally on the verge . . .'

'How do you know they didn't cross the line?'

'Because my mother stopped them. They did not cross that line.'

'As far as you know. So what did they do in the end?'

'They gave back the old lady to the relatives. But they still wanted to keep the money, the inheritance, and the relatives complained and that's when it all blew up. And there was a court case, I think.'

'And did they end up giving up their claim?'

'I don't know. You will have to find out. I can't remember. By then we weren't talking to them . . . I just couldn't . . . We didn't speak to them for years because of this. You see, the trouble was, if you associated with them, you were putting yourself in danger, every time.'

'What, you mean, legally, like an accessory before the fact?'

'Not only that. But if you by any chance said anything, she could use it. Against you.'

'Like how?'

'Let's say you were having an affair, or something, or she knew something very personal . . .'

'Oh yeah, I get it. Like, "If you don't do what I want, I'll tell your husband you are having an affair."'

'Yes.'

But why didn't Ruthie, or her late husband, do something about it? She was married to a marvellous, kind, urbane man called Percy Cohen, who was a professor of sociology at the London School of Economics. Why didn't they tell the police?

'We talked about it. We discussed it. But we didn't go to the police. First of all she was my sister. It would have looked vindictive. And she would have taken me with her. She would have hurt me, badly. And my family.'

'How do you mean?'

'I had one tiff with her, in the fifties. And she made my life a misery for me, for three years after that. You must understand, if we had got involved, she would have run rings around us . . . she was very clever. She used to run rings around the lawyers, all of them. If we had told her that we were going to the police she would have worked out a plan to ruin us, or something. She was very, very clever. And she was frightening. But do you know something? She was also very funny. Very, very funny. And she used her humour as a weapon. Listen. You want to know what she could get up to? Let me tell you a story. You had that place you lived in, in Dorking, yes?'

'Yeah, that's right.'

'Well, they built an extension, and the roof on it was two inches too low for her taste. And she didn't like it. So she said to the builder, "Rebuild it." He of course said, "No." So she said, "If you don't, I'll have your balls on a plate," or something like that. And he said, "I don't care." So she tried a different tack. She knew he was trying to get divorced at the time but he couldn't get shot of his wife. So your mother said, "If I give you good reason to divorce her, will you rebuild the roof for me?" And he said, "Yes." So they managed to persuade the wife to go to a hotel and go upstairs, for some obscure reason, and then sent your father upstairs after her. To make it look like adultery, you see. And they took pictures of her going into the bedroom, and then him, and then the two of them coming out. And so she got screwed completely.'

'What? Literally?'

'No. Financially. Because they had the proof, so to speak, that she had committed adultery, the courts gave her husband the divorce. And she got nothing. All the money she was entitled to, and she got nothing. And the builder rebuilt your mother's extension for her, in return.'

'So what you're saying is, if she could do that to them, she could do it to you.'

'Yes. We were scared, to be honest.'

'But you know what they say . . . "For evil to flourish, it is only necessary for good men to do nothing."'

'Yes, but they also say that blood is thicker than water.'

'So . . . what was it like, looking at me when I was growing up and knowing that my mother was . . . a ruthless person . . . and not telling me?'

'I . . .'

Ruthie's voice began to falter and her eyes began to fill. Until this point I had been talking to her as if she were an interviewee and we were in front of a camera. It was as if the only purpose of the occasion was to extract information and the person being discussed was someone I had never met before. Not any more. The emotion could stay inside me no longer.

'You were away at school, so you were not part of it . . . that horrible . . . boiling pot. Yes, I am sorry, sweetheart, I can see it is very painful for you . . . it is also painful for me. But there was no way I was going to tell you that your mother was cruel, that she had no conscience . . . but you must remember that you had good feelings for your mother and she for you, and those feelings are something to hold on to.'

'But . . . why? She was intelligent. Why wasn't she intelligent enough to know that what she was doing was wrong, even if she had no conscience to tell her that?'

'What made her go like that? I honestly can't tell you. But you know . . . you must understand, there is always temptation in situations like that.'

Ruthie had run old people's homes too, for many years, in north London and Hertfordshire. She got the idea from my mother. She followed in her footsteps in that respect. Not in the other, though. She did, however, sometimes find herself in situations where there were, as she put it, 'thoughts'.

'You are given something valuable to look after, by an old person. It happens all the time. And the thought goes through your head, it always does, just for a second: "Gosh, I could run off with this if I wanted to." But you never do, because your character, your conscience, your morality, whatever, stops you. It's the leap between the temptation, the thought . . . and the actual doing. She made that leap.'

'So what was it about her . . . that made her take that leap?'

'She . . . she had a taste for money. Her hobby was shopping. She went to the shops when she felt like it and she would buy everything. And she used to give away stuff, because she had so much stuff in her house. To make way for more.'

'And all the time she was telling people how good she was at business.'

'In a way that was true. But not that kind of business.'

'The scales are dropping from my eyes. There was me, thinking my mother was a bit of a character, different, eccentric, funny, whatever . . . and now this.'

'Yes, but why do you want to tell this story, in a book, for everyone to know?'

'Well . . . loads of reasons. Actually, one reason, I guess, is to apologize . . . and to try and get rid of the guilt I'm starting to feel.'

'Guilt? It's nothing to do with you! You did not do these things.'

'Well, I do feel it. And shame too.'

'Ah, yes. The sins of the parents.' She then said something completely unintelligible.

'What?' I said.

'It's Hebrew. It means: "The parents will eat the bitter fruit and the teeth of the children will vanish." It is biblical. It means that the parents commit the sins, and the misery of the sins, the misery and the shame, is visited on their children.'

She then wrote down the Hebrew for me on the back of the will: *Avot achloo boser veshiney banim tikhena.*

'Thanks for this,' I said, staring at what she had written.

A bunch of letters that, a few seconds ago, would have been entirely meaningless now carried more meaning than I could possibly comprehend at this point. I tried saying them myself.

'*Avot achloo boser veshiney banim tikhena.*What a lovely thought to have on a Monday morning.'

We hugged each other and said goodbye. I had no doubt whatsoever that she had been telling me the truth. I had only to see the look on her face both during and after our talk to know that.

13 February 1987

Was a Monday. I had just finished breakfast at 20 Egmont Road and was getting ready to leave. I was due in at Radio Bristol that afternoon. I should really have driven down to the West Country the night before but I didn't fancy it. I was taking my things out to the car when the phone rang. Pat, my mother's alcohol-friendly cleaner, answered it. It was the hospital, she said. They wanted to speak to a member of the family. I can't remember feeling much emotion when the woman at the other end told me she was dead. I was on autopilot immediately. That's what a lot of people do, isn't it? I thanked the person who'd called and then rang my news editor at Radio Bristol. I told her I wouldn't be in for work that day. I clearly wasn't making much sense because she started saying that they really needed me in that day and was I sure I couldn't make it? I explained again what had happened and she spluttered an embarrassed apology.

22 August 2005

leave for America soon so I have been tying up some loose ends. I rang Jean Stern, Jack's distant relative, to see whether she had made any headway with her enquiries. She had said she would ask her cousin – an authority on all Stern-related issues – whether he could shed any light on the matter. She had – but he couldn't.

'I haven't found out anything more, I'm afraid, young man.'

'So not even your cousin could help?'

'No . . . you see, it's rather a distant relationship, none of us really knew Uncle Jack.'

'Poor old Jack . . . he was pretty much out on his own, wasn't he?'

'Yes, he was. I can't help you. Have you managed to find out anything? Is there anything to worry about?'

'From my point of view, quite a lot. But it's all a bit late now.'

'Oh, I see. Well, you know . . . they've all died! It's such a bore! We should have asked them all while they were alive, you know.'

'We certainly should.'

Then it was my new septuagenarian lawyer friends.

Humphrey in France, Bruce in Oxshott. Both had been sniffing about – or, in Humphrey's case, had asked someone else to do the sniffing about for him – and found nothing in the ledger cards to suggest that there was any court case, or litigation, over old Mr Stern's will. It was, therefore, 99.9 per cent certain that my mother claimed the money 'due' to her under his will.

Next up I called Dennis in Malaga. He was helping out a neighbour with his gardening and had just been stung by a wasp, he told me. Apparently Spanish wasps hurt a lot more than British ones. I had to tread reasonably carefully. I knew he still harboured very fond memories of my mother, despite every-thing, and I didn't want to ruin them. But I also wanted to find out whether he'd been telling me the whole truth when I was out there, without accusing him of having (understandably) lied to me. I started by telling him what I knew about the Stern case. He said that he recognized the name. He and my mother had actu-ally talked about it. She never went into detail, he said, but she had told him that there were problems with the Stern will. 'I think she told me that he made his will out to her, yeah . . . but that was because of how wonderfully she'd looked after him . . . but I never knew anything about borrowing money off of him, or anything like that.'

I wondered aloud whether he was withholding any informa-tion just to protect my feelings.

'Nah, nah . . . I'd never cover up anything, Jonny. Not then and not now. Most of the things I had anything to do with were these planning problems she had, that stuff. Nothing like this.'

'This is a different league altogether.'

'It certainly sounds like it. She never got up to anything like that when she was with me. If she had I'd have been right out of there. She used to blame everything on your dad, though . . . used to say she had to keep him in check.'

'In what way?'

'Oh, like she had to stop him double-charging the residents, stuff like that. They would pay by standing order and he would go round copping cheques off of 'em, as well.'

'So she blamed him . . . I wonder if he'll blame her.'

'You'd better get over there quick, hadn't you.'

'I better had.'

23 August 2005

I got a timely reminder this morning, not that I needed it, of what might have happened back in the sixties if the authorities had been more proactive. The producer of *House of Horrors* told me about a great story we're featuring in the next series. A builder in Essex – we'll call him Mr D – has been systematically ripping off old people for huge sums of money. Tomorrow, the police are going to arrest him at the home of one of his victims: a pensioner who was persuaded/cajoled/conned by Mr D into signing over the deeds of his house to him. The con would have made Mr D around £50,000 if it had worked. Thankfully it didn't, owing mainly to Trading Standards and the fact that our pensioner is still alive and able to give evidence. It made me realize, not for the first time, what was so cunning about my mother's modus operandi in the Stern case. It would have been nigh on impossible to prove, conclusively, that she was guilty of theft, extortion or whatever, given that there were only three key witnesses, one of whom – Mr Stern – would have been dead or incapable of giving evidence in any trial. The other two witnesses – Mr and Mrs Maitland – would of course have been reluctant, to say the least, to give evidence against each other.

I've also been having a nagging feeling that won't go away about Joan, the daughter of old Mr Stern. None of her relatives – not the ones I've spoken to, anyway – know where she is or what state she's in. Reading between the lines, it's clear they don't even know whether she's still alive or not. I can't stop thinking about the fact that a large amount of money which should – and probably would – have gone to Joan went to my mother instead. So this afternoon I had another go on the Internet to try to track her down. And it worked. I came across something called the Joan Stern Charitable Trust. It is run by a firm of solicitors in the West Country. A phone call to the lawyer in charge of it, a bloke in his sixties called Colin Russell, established that, yes, this Joan Stern was indeed the Joan Stern I was looking for. I asked him whether Joan was still alive.

'Yes, she was taken into a mental home in Galloway in Scotland, a very nice one, at the age of fourteen or so. And there she remains.'

'What kind of a state is she in now?'

'Well, she is eighty-nine. And extremely . . . passive. She just sits there getting old. She has had a mental age of fourteen, or fifteen, for most of her life really.'

'Do people visit her?'

'Yes. I go and see her. And a few distant cousins.'

'What, so . . . friends, members of the family?'

'Well, that's it, you see . . . there aren't any near members of the family. Her mother was actually the heir to a huge whisky fortune, but she died young. So she was brought up by her grandparents in this absolutely enormous pile, this vast great Scottish country house. That ended up with her brother, Eddie, who sold it. Very nice chap, Eddie. But he never had children. Because there was mental instability in the family. And I seem to remember his father had mental instability too. In fact, I think he committed suicide.'

'What? John James Stern committed suicide? I don't think so.'

'Well, my recollection is that he did . . . but I may be quite wrong.'

'Just about Joan again . . . she isn't short of money, is she, anything like that?'

'Oh no. Rather to the contrary. She had an enormous amount of money when she was younger and the courts decided it would be a good idea if a trust was set up to put the money to good use, so that's where I come in. I administer it. I'm not sure she knew much about it at the time, as it was done through the Court of Protection. But she is fine, Joan . . . as fine as she can be, anyway.'

Well, that's something. It doesn't change the nature of what my mother did: it doesn't make it any more, or less, forgivable. But it is marginally comforting to know that Joan has never wanted for anything all her life and that she has been well looked after all these years. And that she has lived all her life serenely unaware that, more than forty years ago, she was cheated out of her rightful inheritance.

I leave for America tomorrow.

26 August 2005

I write this in Room 138 of the Best Western Motel on Pacific Highway Boulevard in Long Beach, California. Long Beach is about 40 miles south of Los Angeles and is its ugly sister: soulless (even by American standards), industrial and scuzzy. It is, however, as the name suggests, by the sea. Which means that today, while downtown Los Angeles has a tarmac-melting 110 degrees Fahrenheit to look forward to, we here in Long Beach are smugly preparing to enjoy a much more endurable afternoon in the mid-eighties. My father and his second wife Doreen met me at LA airport yesterday lunchtime. The procedure was identical to our last four reunions, which have taken place at (roughly) five-yearly intervals. She spots me first: we kiss. She points him out, 20 feet away, with a trolley. He always has a trolley. He likes to be prepared. He is, yet again, wearing his regulation outfit of knee-length cream shorts with an extremely high waistband that serves only to amplify his solid but extraordinarily ample girth. His long white socks are pulled up as far as they can go and are accompanied by sensible grey shoes. The light-coloured Fred Perry top is tucked neatly into his shorts and he looks, I suddenly realize, like Humpty Dumpty. Facially, he is a cross between an elderly, balding, Fred Flintstone and Ed Asner, the American actor who used to play the title role in the TV series *Lou Grant*. If you haven't heard of him, try Ernest Borgnine. His large, friendly, red face breaks out into a huge smile as soon as he sees me and we hug for about five seconds and then he is off, once he has established that I don't need the trolley, because I have only hand luggage. ('Are you sure, son? I got it specially.') He always does this, I tell Doreen, as we make our way to the car park using his large, waddling bottom 10 yards in front of us as our beacon. Even though we haven't seen each other for years, he only ever allows himself a few seconds' worth of greeting and then, without fail, immediately shoots off into the near-distance, without even bothering to try to start a conversation. She laughs.

'He's not going to change now, is he?' she says. I laugh too. I always laugh when he is around. Sometimes at him, sometimes with him. Having said that, my experience of him has been very limited. I never knew him as a child, as he and my mother got divorced when I was seven. Before that, I was away at boarding school most of the time. Even when I wasn't, he always – like her – seemed to be 'busy with the business'. I saw him a bit after they got divorced but we didn't have a very close relationship. He was never unkind, he just didn't seem that interested. Unlike Dennis, we never did stuff together: I can't ever remember going to see a film with him, attending a soccer match, or even going for a meal. The nearest we got was in the mid-seventies when we were supposed to be going to see Arsenal v. Sheffield United. I was waiting for him to come and pick me up when he phoned an hour before he was due and said that he didn't really want to go after all and couldn't we go off and do something more interesting instead. We couldn't agree on a replacement activity so the whole thing got cancelled and I ended up doing nothing, alone.

He doesn't move too badly for an 80-year-old, I thought, as we neared the car. He may walk like an overweight penguin but at least he doesn't need a stick. Supple, however, he is not. Watching him try to manoeuvre himself into the back seat of the car via the front passenger door was like watching a rhino trying to climb into a foxhole. He laughed about it, though: we all did. He's got a good laugh. A big, dirty cackle. And his way of speaking was, as ever, highly entertaining: a semi-shouted, Jewish cockney accent with traces of Frankie Howerd and an East End fruit and veg seller. And the same old stock phrases. Such as: 'Everything happens for a reason.' Or: 'Everything that doesn't kill you makes you stronger.' And his all-time favourite, delivered as if he's never said it before when in fact I've heard it approximately fifty times: 'Nobody knows what goes on between a man and a woman . . . only God. And sometimes, even he doesn't know.' Indeed. Funny how something can suddenly take on a new meaning when it's heard for the fifty-first time.

Dad and Doreen moved to Long Beach last year after spending more than twenty years living and working in Las Vegas. He used to operate the lift that took people to the top of the highest casino in Nevada, the Stratosphere, and back down again. He used to wear a uniform – bright red jacket, black shirt and black trousers – and, as far as I could tell, enjoyed his job quite a bit. Once, when he was given an employee of the month award, he sent me the relevant page from the staff newsletter. His biggest satisfaction, from what I could gather, was getting one over on his bosses. They had told him he couldn't have his lunch (sandwiches, packed by Doreen) on the job, i.e. in sight of the customers. So he took to eating them in the washroom. But the bosses told him that wasn't allowed either as some customers could still see him and what's more they – the management –

were able to watch the whole thing on CCTV. There was only one thing for it. He started eating his lunch on the lavatory, in a locked toilet cubicle, where absolutely no one, or thing, could see him. If it makes you happy . . .

A few years ago he and Doreen put their names down for two apartments at a sheltered-housing-type place in Long Beach: a kind of hall of residence for senior citizens, complete with janitors, handymen, and very cheap rents. A few months ago two places came up so they both packed up work and moved west. His apartment, which we saw first, was small, clean and virtually devoid of all possessions, apart from a poster of a red number 12 London bus on his bedroom door and a few family photos, including several, I noticed, of my wedding. Doreen's place, which was a few hundred yards away from his in a separate block, was identically sized but had loads more stuff and felt far more homely. It was an interesting set-up, I said to my father, and one that many men would be envious of. Yes, he said. The only problem was that Doreen's apartment, which was five minutes' walk away, wasn't far enough. Cue cackling laughter from him. En route to Doreen's we passed one of the janitors. My father insisted on stopping to speak to him. It's a family trait – one of the few, I think, that we share: I can't resist asking shop assistants, waiters and delivery men where they're from. Unlike him though, I don't start shouting 'Filipino? I LOVE FILIPINOS!' at the top of my voice, once I've found out their country of origin. Quite endearing, really – if a little embarrassing.

We had a cup of tea in Doreen's apartment and I quizzed them both about their lifestyles. His seemed to consist mainly of him walking to her place at 8 a.m. for a bowl of porridge and prunes ('A minimum of eight prunes every morning!') followed by a bit of light walking, TV watching, reading and sleeping, followed by dinner at a local restaurant at six. They asked whether I was going to join them for their evening meal but I declined, citing jet lag. To be honest, I also wanted to get my head together. There were, of course, a million and one questions I wanted to ask: but now clearly wasn't the time.

27 August 2005.

Early this evening we went for a meal at a place called the Roadhouse Grill, a typical American diner about twenty minutes away from my father's apartment. While we were waiting for the food to arrive he told me the story of how he and my mother met. It was quite romantic, really: he heard her voice before he actually saw her face. It was 1945 and he was flying jets for the RAF in what was then Palestine. She was in the air-craft control department of the Women's Auxiliary Air Force. Her job was to talk to the pilots and give them vital information. 'All clear to land on Runway 556' – that kind of thing. One day my mother introduced herself to him shortly after he'd touched down, saying she liked the sound of his voice. Soon after that it became clear that Runway 556 wasn't the only place where he had the all-clear to touch down. Within two years they were married and within three they were on the slow boat to England with their two small kids, Rachel and Maurice. They spent the fifties living in Carshalton, near Sutton, and doing menial jobs – she made dresses and worked for Vernons Pools, he was a super-visor for the Royal Mint. One of his tasks was to make sure none of the men nicked any of the gold coins they were manufacturing there. It wasn't easy: some of them were pretty ingenious. One favoured ruse, apparently, was to wear chewing gum on the soles of your shoes, which would then pick up fair quantities of gold dust off the factory floor. After a spell making tubes for TV sets he got a job working as a manager for Granada cinemas but, my mother decided, there simply wasn't enough money coming into the household, so there was only one thing for it. They would have to let a room.

'That sounds familiar,' I said.

'Yes, actually, the room where you were born was the first one to go. We advertised it and lo and behold an elderly lady turned up with her son. She was about seventy-something, very eccentric. One day I took her breakfast in and there she was in a negligee, lying on the bed, showing off the lot. It was terrible. She took my hand and said, "I need your company".'

'You didn't shag her, did you?'

'Good God no. But Bru wouldn't have minded if I had. She said to me, "You've got to do what she wants, we need the money. Go and borrow some money from her so we can do some building work and start a business." So to cut a long story short, we borrowed the money from this old lady and got another loan off the bank manager and that let us start the old people's home.'

'Did the old lady get her money back?'

'Oh yes, of course, yes. We used to give them interest, up front to start with. So, say we borrowed a thousand pounds, we'd give them interest of a hundred, straight away, and then monthly cheques.'

I was just taking in the significance of the word 'them', as in: 'We used to give them interest, up front', when the food arrived and the tape recorder fell off the table. Given that Doreen was listening to every word and we were on the verge of discussing some extremely sensitive subject matter, I decided that it would be for the best if there were no further questions on this matter, M'lud, for the remainder of the evening. Trouble is, I only have one day left before I return to the UK.

28 August 2005

This evening we went for another of those gargantuan meals the Americans specialize in. Even the cutlery, I noticed, was outsize. After that we went back to the housing complex where my father and Doreen live. I suggested that it might be a good idea if I chatted with Dad a bit in his own flat, as Doreen might find some of his ramblings a bit boring.

'Oh no,' she said, 'don't do that, it's far too hot in his place. Come and do it in mine.'

'But what will you do?' I said. 'It could get a bit tedious.'

'That's OK, I'll stay in the bedroom. You won't hear me.'

Well, it's now or never, I thought. Let's do it.

We set ourselves up for what I assumed was going to be a long and difficult conversation. We sat with our backs to the wall facing the TV screen in Doreen's front room. He was in a reclining armchair and I was right next to him on a two-seater sofa. I angled my body round so we could see each other's faces. I didn't think there was anything to be gained from pussyfooting around so I got straight to the point.

'Now tell me about Mr Stern.'

'Mr Stern? What? The old man we used to look after?'

'Yes ... I've been doing some background work and found out a few interesting things and I just wondered ... what happened with him.'

He didn't looked shocked or surprised.

'Right ... Mr Stern.'

He then did something strange and unexpected. He laughed. Not the full-throated cackle. More of a giggle. I wasn't sure what it signified. It may have been a guilty laugh, or the sweet chuckle of remembrance. Then he went on.

'He was a very nice old man of about eighty-something and he was involved in a posh estate agents called Stern and Parsons. But Bru ... she made me go a bit too far then, to extract money from him, and it bit into his capital. And before we had a chance to give it back, his son found out about it, from looking at his bank statements, I think. So he confronted us about it. But Bru came up with this story that he was forcing the money on her – the old man was – because he fancied her.'

'Because he fancied her?'

'Yes. Very clever. She told the son that the old man, his father, had been paying her to sleep with him.'

'To sleep with him? Had she?'

'No! He was in his eighties and senile, for a start.'

'Right. When in fact you'd been borrowing the money off him ... correct?'

'Yes.'

I checked myself. I had suddenly become aware of a forcefulness in my tone. I didn't want to sound too inquisitorial. But then again this was my only chance to find out from him what really happened. Or rather – pardon me while I take off the hat marked 'son' and put on the one marked 'journalist' – this was my only chance to hear *his* version of events. He didn't seem to mind my line of questioning, however, so I ploughed on.

'How much did you borrow?'

'Oh, a few thousand, I think. Not sure.'

'It's interesting that the son kicked up a fuss. I thought he was rich and he wouldn't have been that bothered or interested in a few thousand quid going missing. But you say he made a stink?'

'Well, yes, he was. Very rich. But he didn't actually kick up a stink, he just queried it. Very aristocratic man.'

'So after Bru came up with her story he didn't take it any farther?'

'Oh no.'

'And there was a bit of business with the will, with Stern, wasn't there?'

My father didn't say anything. It felt a bit awkward. I carried on.

''Cos he . . . signed his will over to Bru.'

'Because he fancied her.'

'But what happened with all that? What went on, with him signing his will over to her, and that?'

'I honestly don't remember that. I really don't. And you know, if I'm not sure about something, I don't want to mislead you. How did you find that out?'

'Well, Rachel remembers you two having a big argument about it, about his will.'

'Really? I don't remember about his will, though.'

''Cos . . . I dug out a copy, from the records . . .'

'You've got a copy of the will?'

'Yeah, I've got a copy of it here.' I gestured to the white plastic laundry bag from my motel room which contained the now rather dog-eared copy of the Stern will, along with my wallet, my mobile and some audio tapes. I continued.

'And in it, he left everything to Bru.'

'Did he? How much was that?'

'Twenty grand.'

He made an odd noise, a cross between a laugh and a splutter.

'That must have been the car she bought for me then. Once I went off to Amsterdam, and when I came back she was waiting for me at the airport with a new car, a Mercedes sports, lovely metallic silver, a 220SE. I remember she said something like 'Happy birthday, welcome back, look what I've got you'. And there it was, she even had a chauffeur driving it. It was our sixth car at the time – we'd already got a beautiful Mercedes 230SL sports car, a Simca estate car, a Mini . . . a Triumph . . . a Rover.'

He was going off the point.

'I think you may have got the timing wrong actually, Dad. She got left this Stern money *after* you were divorced, so she would-n't have spent it on a car for you, would she? Let's just go back a bit. What about the will?'

'The will? My God. No, I didn't know that.'

It felt like the right time to produce the key evidence. I fished around in the white plastic laundry bag. That noise again – the laugh-cum-splutter. He asked me to pass him his reading glasses from the coffee table in front of us and he began studying the papers.

'But didn't the son contest this?'

'No. There's absolutely no record of it, anyway. I mean, if he had contested it, in court or anywhere else, I would have found out about it by now. And you would have known about it at the time, quite possibly.'

'She might have paid him off.'

'Possibly. I do know she was warned by Benson and Co. not to take the money. But I doubt whether she would have taken much notice.'

'Oh no. She would never have listened to them. She would have done exactly the opposite of what they told her to do.'

'And maybe, if the son did make a fuss, she just gave him the story about the sex and all that and he would have just gone away and not made a fuss.'

'Quite possibly. She was very clever, you know.'

He carried on poring over the will. When he got to the bit where the executors had signed, he started murmuring.

'Ah, yes . . . Bruce Carter . . . Humphrey Benson . . . very nice people.'

I wanted to bring him back to the key point. The actual signing of the will. He appeared to know nothing about it. But Rachel said she clearly remembered our parents arguing about whether or not Stern should be made to sign. I didn't want to accuse my father of being a liar but I wanted to make sure that I had at least tested his story, if not to destruction. It was my turn to splutter.

'But . . . what can you remember, 'cos you . . . you know, you got him to lend money to Bru and all that, but what about this, 'cos Rachel remembers you and her having a really bad argument and her saying to you, "Look, get him to sign, get him to sign the will." And that you were very distressed about it.'

'But my name isn't on there, anywhere, is it?' he said, pointing to the will.

'No. It isn't. But it doesn't have to be. Just 'cos it's not there doesn't mean you didn't . . .'

I paused, trying to work out where I should take it next. He spoke again.

'She used to get me to get him to sign cheques over to us, for sure. But I don't remember the will. I didn't even know about that at all.'

'Really? Didn't you?'

'No!' He laughed again. 'Cor! You're very clever, getting hold of that.'

'It wasn't that difficult. Listen . . .'

He suddenly changed the subject and started repeating what he'd been telling me a few minutes earlier.

'Oh yes, listen, she had a chauffeur in that Mercedes, very nice young man, him and his wife, she took on both of them, then she went and fired them the next day. But it was very extravagant, we didn't need that car, we really didn't.'

'Fine, but about the will. I know she borrowed money off Stern before he died. Then, because he left everything to her in his will . . .'

He nipped in and finished off my sentence before I had a chance to do so myself.

'She didn't have to pay it back.'

'Correct. Which meant that all her debts were forgiven.'

'That's right.'

'So it obviously made sense to get him to sign the lot over . . .'

'It does makes sense. She's a very clever woman, isn't she.'

'Well . . . she was, then. What was Stern's state of mind back then?'

'He was a bit senile. He was a very lovely person. But he really wasn't all there.'

'And how did you feel about getting him to sign the cheques and stuff?'

'I didn't . . . erm . . . agree. But . . . you know . . . I suppose I had to do what she wanted, because she enticed me, you know.'

I asked him how she managed to do that and my father replied. Suffice to say it had something to do with lipstick and hair removal.

'But . . . didn't you say, "Look, this is bad, we shouldn't be borrowing money from old people . . ."?'

'Yes. But she said, "You do it or else."'

'Or else what?'

'Well, she was a bit mad. I mean, you know, you didn't know what she was going to do.'

'What? Like, leave you, or kill you?'

'One or the other. Yeah. Easily.'

'Really?'

'Yeah. Well, I wouldn't worry about her killing me, 'cos I probably would have killed her first. But we were so involved with everything, with work, I was working very, very hard, I was running the homes and doing the shopping and looking after the staff and doing the admin . . .'

'Sure, I know it would have been difficult. But look . . . how hard would it have been to have turned round and said, "Look, you can't borrow money off senile old blokes"? Did you try saying that?'

'I did. Yes, I did. Of course.'

'And?'

'Well, she just said, "We've got to do it, for the children's future, for their education." And she had committed us to so many debts and things, that was the only way I could think of, to pay the debts back. She was always shopping for things we didn't need, like many thousands of pounds' worth of Mercedes, and all sorts of things.'

'But did you really try talking her out of it? Out of getting money off the old people?'

'Yes, of course I did, but it was no good . . . you couldn't speak to her, she was very difficult, half bloody madwoman. Ha.'

I was still troubled about the Stern will. How could he not have known about it? It was, after all, made and signed in 1965, when he and Bru were still very much married to each other and running the business together. They were a very close team. How on earth, I asked, did he not know about it? Was he absolutely sure he couldn't remember?

'Well . . . right . . . maybe *she* got him to sign it. I honestly don't remember asking him to sign a will.' He appeared to have lost some of his earlier certainty. He continued:

'I can remember him signing cheques, but I can't remember him signing a will. Give me those glasses again.'

'Sure,' I said. 'It might jog your memory.'

I handed him his reading glasses from the coffee table and he began scouring the will yet again.

'I'm sure I wasn't involved in this. Maybe I was away when it happened.'

'But Rachel says she distinctly remembers the conversation you two had about it. She said you were very upset about it. Maybe it was so traumatic it just slipped from your memory . . .'

'I don't know. I doubt it.'

It was time to move on. I wanted to explore his modus operandi at the time.

'And what was your method of getting these people, like Stern, to sign cheques? Did you do the charm bit, and crack a few jokes? Because the preferred method now is to be strong and assertive, you know. Take command, be manipulative. Rude, even. Tell them their sofa doesn't go with their curtains.'

He looked confused. I realized he probably didn't know what I was talking about. Not surprising, really. I didn't bother explaining what I meant. I was just trying to make him a bit more comfortable as I sensed he was feeling uneasy. I was still trying, perhaps unsuccessfully, not to be too aggressive: he was my father, after all. And he was eighty years old. I tried a different tack.

'What I mean is . . . how did you persuade them?'

'Well, I used to tell them the truth. I used to say, "Look, my wife needs the money because she needs it for school fees and to expand the business and all that. And if you lend it to us, it will

give you a better mode of living and a better room and so on."
And then we would give them money upfront, as interest.'

He paused for a moment.

'And, well, I suppose they coughed up because they were
scared, too.'

'Scared? Of what?'

'Scared of being thrown out.'

'Did she not express any kind of guilt?'

'No. Never. On the contrary. On no. Definitely not.'

'And did you ever feel bad?'

'I always felt bad, because I felt it was unnecessary. I didn't see
the point in it. We were doing very well, we were earning good
money, everything was going nicely. But then she would exceed
herself . . . she was very greedy, you see, and whatever we had,
she wanted more. So she would go out and buy more and
commit us to more and more debt. And she said we had to keep
expanding, or we weren't going to get anywhere.'

'But haven't you ever thought about what you've done since?
Don't you have any regrets about what you did?'

'I don't really have any regrets about my life, Jonny. Because
everything that was done . . . seemed to be right at the time.
You know, I was very happy with her as a wife and a
mother . . . and I just felt I had to go along with her. And I am
very loyal and faithful, you know. There was no point in arguing with her. And she used to make out that it was reasonable,
what was happening.'

'But what happened to your sense of right and wrong?'

'At the time . . . there was nothing wrong in it, as far as I
was concerned. We were borrowing money off the people we
were looking after and we had a very good reputation at the
time.'

'Well, hold on . . . these were very vulnerable, potentially scared old people. The last thing you should be doing, if you are looking after them, is borrowing money off them.'

'Well, it was done with a lot of other old people's homes at the time.'

'Was it?'

'Oh yes, our good friends the O'Callaghans. They used to borrow money off their old people. And they used to mistreat them, too. Lock 'em up in their rooms and not feed them and things like that.That's why there were always these inspectors going round.'

'Well, it doesn't make it right, does it?'

It was time to move on. To another grubby allegation.

'And what about the drama of the old lady, the one you took to stay at our own house in Dorking and the relatives got pissed off, and you were keeping her in the . . .'

'Attic?'

'Yes, and you charged her loads of rent and stuff and there was a court case maybe . . .'

'Well, yes, there was a threat of a court case . . . but there wasn't an actual court case. The woman's cousin was a JP, a Justice of the Peace, you see. I can't remember the exact name, it may have been Carney or Carrick or something like that.'

'So what happened there?'

'Well, I think he threatened to have us taken to court, so she . . . paid up . . . you know, paid him off.'

'What . . . you mean, she paid back the money that you had borrowed off her?'

'Yes, that's right.'

'And did Mum give up her claim on the old lady's will?'

'She wasn't in her will . . . not as far as I know, anyway.'

'But she could have been.'

'She could have been . . . but the cousin, this JP, he was a very determined man so I don't think he would have stood for that.'

It was time for the subject matter to get even more delicate. I told him what Ruthie had told me. That Bru was desperate to make the scandal go away. That her mother was staying with my father and Bru at the time. That Bru had suggested that there was 'a way to make this go away . . . for good'.

What did he know about this? I asked. And was she capable of actually doing such a thing, rather than just talking about it? He remained silent for a few seconds.

'Yeah . . . she would be capable of mur . . . of murder, you mean? Yes, she would be.'

'How do you know?'

'Well, because her mind was unbalanced. If she wanted something, she would go to any lengths to get it. She nearly killed Ruthie once, in a fight over one of her mother's diamond rings, after she had died. And she once asked me to get rid of Dennis for her.'

'What?'

He fell quiet for a while, unsure whether to finish what he had started.

'Well . . . I only tell you this because you ask what she was capable of, but she once asked me to come and see her when she was in hospital. Some time in the early seventies, I think. And she asked me to get someone to have Dennis bumped off. She knew that I was a member of the Freemasons, you see, and she thought I could do it that way.'

'And did you?'

'Good God no! I wanted to have nothing to do with it.'

'But was she serious?'

'Definitely.'

'So did you ever discuss with her about how to get rid of this old lady, then, Carney, Carrick, whatever?'

'No ... no ... I never heard that at all. She was always in close cahoots with her mother, I know that.'

'So how did it all go away in the end, then?'

'Well, the cousin, the JP, he didn't take it to court but he reported it to the local council, and they took the licence away. The licence you need from the local authorities to run old people's homes.'

'Right. Aha. I see, I see. So that's why all your places were closed down.'

'Yes.'

Bingo. That's one mystery solved, then.

'Was there a bit of a stink at the time?' I asked.

'What do you mean?'

'It must have caused a bit of a scandal. In the press, I mean.'

'Oh yes, it was in the papers. A man from the local paper in Epsom came to my flat in Lancaster Gate, where I was living after the divorce, and asked me a few questions. So I gave him some quotes.'

'What did you say?'

'That we had done nothing wrong.'

'And what about the authorities – the police and stuff. Did they get involved?'

'Yes, I got asked a few questions by the CID in Epsom.'

'What? You were taken in for questioning by the police?'

'No, they came to me.'

'What happened?'

'Nothing. They didn't charge me with anything because they had nothing to charge me with.'

'Right. OK. Erm ... let's move on to the next thing. How many people did she get you to borrow money from?'

'Oh, a lot. Er ... Sir David Brink, he was a very good man, an adviser to the government, I think ... then there was Dr

Grove . . . he was paralysed, he had a daughter who was an alcoholic... a Miss Smithson, she was a retired schoolteacher . . . the
old lady I told you about in the first place, Mrs Orrish. About
six, I think.'

'What kind of sums are we talking about?'

'I think it varied . . . between five hundred and a couple of
thousand.'

In today's money, that's anything from two to twenty thousand pounds.

'And were they all paid back? Or did some of them just die in
the meantime?'

'No, they were always paid back.'

'Are you sure? 'Cos Stern wasn't, for a start.'

'Well, no, evidently not, ha ha ha ha. But no, we always made
standing orders, in favour of the people we were supposed to be
paying back.'

'Well, that's as maybe. But if Stern wasn't paid back – and he
wasn't – how do you know the others weren't, either?'

He allowed himself a few seconds of contemplation. For the
first time in the conversation I became aware of Doreen doing
something at the breakfast bar at the other end of the room. I
had forgotten she was there. She couldn't hear what we were
saying.

'Well . . . I don't know. I mean, we had a joint account, so she
could easily have stopped them being repaid. Yes, she could have
stopped the money from our bank going to them.'

There were other allegations to put to him. What about the
supposed double charging? Did residents really pay twice, once
by standing order and then again by cheque? It was possible,
he said. It may have been that he turned a blind eye when a resident overpaid, because he felt that he and Bru needed the
money. He was far more definitive, however, on another point.

In fact he volunteered the information; I didn't even have to ask.

'What she would do, if one of the old women peed in bed, say, was send a bill for a heavy amount of money to her relatives, saying that that particular woman was incontinent, and because we weren't a nursing home, we would have to charge extra for cleaning and all that. She would just make things up.'

'Like what? Is this the shitty mattress trick?'

'Yes, she would use the same mattress and say, look, your old boy or whatever has shat on it and you've got to pay for it.'

'How much?'

'Oh, ridiculous sums of money.'

'And how did you feel about that?'

'Rotten. But . . . I had the admin to do, I had to pay for all her debts, I was caught up in her . . . quagmire, her vicious circle, her web. I was happy running the homes and doing the work, the physical work and the mental work, so I was content and happy and I just wanted it to carry on that way. So I just had to go along with her. That was terrible, that mattress business, really.'

'But how did you live with that and all the other stuff? Didn't you have any sleepless nights, or did you just learn to live with the guilt? 'Cos in a way, you were her . . .'

'Accomplice.'

'Exactly.'

'Yeah . . . well, maybe I enjoyed it . . . you know, if you can't beat them, join them. Ha ha ha ha.'

'What, you mean if you can't beat her, join her?'

'Yes, that's right.'

I could see he was getting tired. I started putting stuff back in the white plastic laundry bag. As I picked up the copy of Stern's will I noticed some human handwriting on the back. It was the old Hebrew saying that Aunt Ruthie had told me. *Avot achloo boser veshiney banim tikhena.* 'The parents will eat the bitter fruit and the teeth of the children will vanish.' I said nothing. He suddenly became a little agitated and more lively than he had been throughout our conversation.

He was now very sure of himself.

'Tell me, Jonny. Tell me this. If you love Emily as much as I loved your mother – and I'm sure you do – and she asked you to do something that you didn't think was right, or immoral, you don't know how you would react, do you?'

I thought about it.

'No. No, you're absolutely right. I wouldn't. I don't know for sure how I'd react, no. I like to think I would behave a certain way but I don't know for sure.'

'And then, if you felt very conscientious and righteous and said, "No, I'm not going to go along with this," and then she said, "Well, OK, I'm leaving you," how would you react then?'

'No, fair enough. I see your point.'

'You would throw your morals out the window and go along with her. You'd say what I said, which was, "Well, I love her, she's all I've got, I don't know what else to do. And what's the worst that can happen if I do go along with her?" I weighed it all up and I didn't see any risks. I mean, I wasn't a dummy and I knew what we could get away with.'

'Do you ever think about it now, then?'

'Well . . . what's done is done. It's gone, it's water under the bridge, isn't it?'

'Maybe your problem was that she was immoral and you were amoral. And together you made an unfortunate combination.'

'Yes, maybe.'

My father shrugged. He seemed remarkably untroubled by our conversation. He looked content and at peace and had a beatific smile. I, meanwhile, felt exhausted and mildly traumatized. I found it hard to reconcile the sweet look on his face with some of the things he had just told me. But there would be plenty of time for me to try to work it out. Like the next thirty years.

29 August 2005

I write this on flight BA279 from Los Angeles to London. I haven't come to any firm conclusions yet about my conversations with my father. I have, though, as you would expect, been churning it all over in my mind. One thing I've been trying to establish, to satisfy my own curiosity as much as anything else, is what part – if any – my father played in the saga of the Stern will. It may be that he had nothing to do with it. It may be that Rachel's memory has been deceiving her and that, for instance, the argument she overheard between them all those years ago was about my father getting a resident to sign a cheque, not a will. Then again, it may well be that she recalled everything exactly as it happened and that my father has simply forgotten – either genuinely or conveniently – what part he played. In the end, I suppose, it doesn't really matter. We know that Bru got Stern to sign the will: the only question mark is whether she did everything herself or got my father to do the dirty work for her. But that's a mere detail, I guess, when you look at the totality of the wrongdoing as a whole. In fact, let me rephrase that last sentence. It's a mere detail when you look at the totality of the wrongdoing that I know about, so far . . .

My father's defence seems to be twofold: that he was, to use the time-honoured excuse, only obeying orders. And that also, if he didn't do what she wanted, she would leave him and he would lose everything. I don't want to judge him at this stage. But people have always said that there was something odd about him: that there seemed to be something missing. Maybe it was a conscience. Whatever he did or didn't do, he is clearly not suffering any guilt about it now. He is basically a content person: and I envy him that. I could see it when I looked at his face as we were driving to the airport a few hours ago. I am glad about that. When we said goodbye at LAX and I was about to disappear through the security gates I turned round to take a last look at him. I knew – and he did – that it might be the last time we would see each other. True to form, he had already turned away and was off into the distance.

5 September 2005

One of the (many) things nagging away at me since I got back has been, oddly, my father's reference to the local paper. He seemed sure that the business about Twin Gables closing down had been in the local press. Had it, though? I found nothing when I went through all those papers, during my marathon microfilm reading session at Sutton Library. I don't like living with the thought that I may have missed something, so last night I looked at my notes again. I quickly realized I had 'done' the box marked 'Epsom and Ewell Advertiser 1966–68', but not the one marked '1969–71'. So this morning I went back to Sutton. It didn't take long. There, in the *Epsom and Ewell Herald* of Thursday, 27 February 1969, on the front page, was a one-column story, with no byline, with the headline: 'OLD FOLK'S HOME REGISTRATION CANCELLED'.

The cancellation of the registration of an old people's home, Twin Gables in London Road, Ewell, has been ordered by an Epsom District Council committee following investigation of a 'grave complaint'.

The following was stated in a report by the Health and

Welfare Committee, which was presented to the Council on
Tuesday: 'Mr and Mrs Maitland, by reason of their treatment of
an elderly person while in their care at their home in Ewell and
at their private residence in Dorking are not fit persons to carry
on a home for old persons and so the Council have ordered that
the registration of Twin Gables be cancelled.'

Mr Irving Maitland, 44, who runs the home with his ex wife
(now Mrs Bru Warrenner) said this week from his home in
Lancaster Gate, London, that he was considering an appeal.
Asked whether Twin Gables had been closed, Mr Maitland said:
'Not at the moment. People are falling over backwards to get in.
This victimisation will only harm the old people.'

This, I am reasonably confident, is what the hack with the
florid complexion was talking about all those months ago, outside Lewes magistrates' court. The dates fit: the hack appears to
be in his late fifties but at the time this story was printed he
would have been in his early twenties – just the right age for a
trainee on a local paper. He may even have been the reporter
who wrote the story and who doorstepped my father at
Lancaster Gate. If, thirty-six years on, he had known what effect
his random moment of recovered memory was going to have on
my life, would he still have said what he said? I wonder. I'm glad
he did say something, though. At least, I think I am.

27 February 1987

My mother was dead. She had died. There was her coffin, right in front of me, being taken out of the back of a hearse by four pall-bearers. Just at that moment the local rabbi, who we'd asked to take the funeral service, asked whether he could have a word with me and Maurice. Our mother had shown not the slightest interest in becoming an Orthodox Jew since the day she set foot in England, but when she was on her deathbed she started talking about seeing a rabbi. So we had no hesitation in asking the Sutton and Cheam synagogue to send along one of their finest for the big day. Before he could take the service however, there was business to attend to. His tone was brisk and unapologetic.

'You offered me fifty pounds but my normal rate is one hundred pounds,' he said, 'and I cannot really go on with this unless you agree to pay me the full rate.'

Looking back, I wish we'd refused and told him where to stick it. But it didn't seem like the time or the place for a stand-up row so we meekly surrendered to his demands. We had been held to ransom by a ruthless, money-grabbing rabbi. My mother would have approved, I guess.

Even at twice the price, though, he was value for money – I'll give him that. In his speech he gave a convincing impression of someone who had known her intimately all his life, even though he had never set eyes on her. All he had to go on was a couple of short midweek briefings on the phone. No one cottoned on, though.

'She was no ordinary woman . . . she lived life . . . and what a life it was . . .' and so on. I sat several rows back, just a few seats along from Dennis. He sobbed steadily into his handkerchief from the moment her coffin was brought in, right through until the end of the service. That's when they played her favourite song, 'This Guy's In Love With You', by Herb Alpert.

My father, who had emigrated to America by this time, wasn't there. I don't know why. I'm not even sure he sent a card. About fifty people turned up, including my Aunt Ruthie, who tearfully embraced the rabbi after it was all over. 'That was her! Exactly! You got her exactly!' she told him. Not quite he hadn't.

1 February 2006

Soon after I saw my sister for the first time in eighteen years, she left a message on my answerphone. 'If you are going to do this properly, Jonny,' she said, 'then you are going to have to tell the full story. You will have to ask our father for all the names of all the people who left money to our mother. After all, if it happened once it could easily have happened several times . . . you need to get all their names and follow them all up.' The same thought had occurred to me too. But I don't want to go any farther down that road. Picking at this shoddy little scab in our family history has been unpleasant and traumatic enough: I'm not that much of a masochist. I'm also, to be honest, afraid of what I might find if I go digging any further.

There were a good many contradictory emotions swirling around inside me when I began writing this book last year. The excitement of chasing down a remarkable story. The increasing sense of horror when I began to realize the full extent of what had gone on. The shame and the guilt of it all, followed by the anger. If I was American I would have acquired squatter's rights on a psychiatrist's couch by now. Today, six months after my last click of the keyboard, I think I can put it into some kind of perspective. For a start, to borrow a phrase from the Fine Young Cannibals, I'm not the man I used to be. By the time I had finished my journey, and this book, my world had turned on its axis. It was a profound shock and unexpectedly disorienting to find out that my mother was not the person I thought she was. I spent twenty-seven years on this earth with her and thought I knew her inside out. Now, nearly twenty years after her death, I've found I didn't know her properly at all. To be a formidable, charismatic, occasionally irrational extrovert is one thing; to be the woman I have now discovered she was is quite another. As a result, all the pieces of my own identity, the things that tell me who I am and what I came from, have been thrown up in the air. And they haven't quite come back down yet. That disorientation makes itself felt in small, seemingly insignificant ways. I feel as if I've misled people. I can't stop thinking about my wedding, two years ago, when I made an emotional speech about what a remarkable woman my mother was and told funny stories about her. People laughed. If I knew then what I know now, I wouldn't have said anything; or if I had, I would have put it quite differently. Now, sadly, when people ask me about her, I change the subject. Or simply tell them the truth. No more funny stories, that's for sure.

Friends and relatives have told me that I shouldn't feel guilty about what my mother and father did. I disagree. How can I not? I directly benefited from it all, for goodness' sake. It was money from the likes of dear old Mr Stern which enabled me to have a top-class private education. The way I see it, somebody has to feel guilt for what happened. That much is owed. Trouble is, I don't think my mother felt any guilt and I don't think my father feels any either, so I'm doing it for them.

It's left a permanent stain – a human stain – on our family. I can't erase it but I can at least try to understand it. And believe me, I've spent a lot of time trying to do just that. Not a day has gone by, since I started this book, when I haven't thought about it. I now realize what she was up to: she was using the kind of win-at-all-costs tactics she tried on me and my siblings on the old people in her care. The only thing at stake in our arguments with her was pride and emotional sanity; but she was playing for far greater stakes with the old people. I wish I'd known.

There are many words I can use to describe what she did but that would be pointless at this stage. All I would say is that I truly feel that just because someone does very bad things, it does not make them a very bad person, period. It is more complex than that. It just makes them a human being who is capable of doing very bad things. My mother did a lot of good things, too: she often showed great generosity – using her own money – to a lot of people, many of whom she hardly knew. I just think her personality traits were magnified. Like the girl in the rhyme, when she was good she was very very good, but when she was bad she was horrid. I can't defend what she did, but I can try and explain it: I think the lure of easy money made her lose sight of what was right and what was wrong. I think she was very good at self-delusion and managed to convince herself that she was justified in doing what she did to Mr Stern, for example, on the basis that he and his relatives had no need of the money anyway. And she would no doubt have thought that she was due more, financially, given the round-the-clock care and attention she was providing him with. And as she said to my brother, on her deathbed, his family had more than enough money anyway. All these 'reasons' are absolute rubbish, of course. But you must indulge me. I'm just trying to make sense of it all.

In some ways I feel sorry for my father: I don't think he was a bad man. I believe, I think, that he was telling the truth when he said he had a terrible choice: to willingly acquiesce in wrong-doing or lose his family and the woman he loved. Tragically, for him, he ended up doing both anyway. Having said that, it's worth remembering that my mother isn't around to defend her-self. If she was, I dare say she would be shovelling the blame for much of what happened back on to my father. I like to think that if I'd been in his position, back in the sixties, I would have blown the whistle, or at least refused to do what was being asked of me. We all would, I suppose. But until we have been in that situation we will never truly know, so don't be too hard on him. One thing that has exercised me greatly, however, is the relationship between my mother and my father. This is a terri-ble thing to say about your parents, but they made an unfortunate combination. I keep thinking about Bonnie and Clyde, Macbeth and Lady Macbeth, and others. Individually, they weren't a problem. Together, they were. They set off some-thing in each other. The partnership's total capacity for wrongdoing far exceeded the sum of its parts. Because my mother had the body of a weak and feeble woman, she couldn't do it on her own. So she needed, to use my father's words, 'an accomplice'. It's a pity their chemistry wasn't more along the lines of Lennon and McCartney's or Rogers and Hammerstein's. If they could have used what they had together to make music, or find cures for illnesses, the world would have been a better place. Instead, they used it to rip off vulnerable and defenceless old people. The acid test, I guess, is whether my mother and father would have acted differently if they had been with dif-ferent partners. I suspect so. After all, both went on to marry other people and neither partnership, as far as I know, got up to any mischief.

Before I started this book I had noticed an increasingly wor-rying trait in myself: over the past ten years I had been growing

more and more enamoured of, and excited by, money. Not
enough for it to have the same corrupting influence on me as it
did on my mother, but enough for it to become more of a moti-
vating force than it perhaps should have been. This particular
apple fell well within the span of the tree. But writing this book
has moved the fruit beyond the branches. The root of all evil,
indeed. I am now all too aware of the power of money and the
consequences that can follow when you want too much of it.
Only the other day a shopkeeper made a mistake and gave me
excess change, thinking I'd given him a twenty-pound note
instead of a tenner. I realized the mistake only when I was out on
the street. I immediately turned on my heels and paid him back.
Time was when I would have thought twice.

This hasn't been a depressing experience, however – far from
it. I'm glad I found out what happened. There is something satisfying about knowing the truth. There is a primal urge in all of
us – maybe it's our consciences – that takes succour from knowing what really went on, even if it was deeply unpleasant. I
suppose I know myself better now. I think that's a good thing.
All those self-help books seem to think it is. Also, I'm in touch
with my brother and sister now, and I wasn't before. If this was
a Mills and Boon job, I'd be telling you that we are now joyously
reconciled and speak lovingly to one another every other day.
But we don't. Our family – and quite possibly yours, too; I'm not
trying to make out that we are anything special – is much too
complex and flawed to live happily ever after. Real life, in my
experience anyway, just isn't like that. You can't not speak to
someone for eighteen years and then expect your relationship to
be exactly the same as it was before, just like that. But I am at
least communicating with my siblings now, which is a vast
improvement.

One of the handful of deep ironies in this book concerns my

relationship with my sister. We became estranged after an argument over money. More specifically, over a will. Our mother's. It all seems very petty and demeaning now – to have argued over relatively insignificant amounts of money while a parent's corpse is barely cold – but as many readers of this book will know, it happens all too often. In our defence, it wasn't just about money. It was about fairness and respecting what each of us believed our mother's final, formal wishes to be. But that was a long time ago now. When I saw my sister again she started to bring it up and tried to justify what had happened. She had no need to. I have forgotten it all. All that remains now, as I say, is the sense of fatalistic irony. It was a will, and my mother, which tore our family apart eighteen years ago. Those same two things have brought us back closer together again.

After reading the manuscript of this book my wife asked, not for the first time, a question that several others have put to me over the years. It was, in effect, 'how come you're so normal – relatively speaking – after growing up with a mother like that?' Or to put it another way, How to Survive Your Mother?

The answer is simple: the same as everyone else does. I'm sorry to repeat, for the millionth time, the Phillip Larkin cliché, but yes, they really do fuck you up, your mum and dad. They really do. It's just a question of how much. In my case I survived, ironically, by being sent away to boarding school and having a circle of close, well-adjusted and down-to-earth friends. And luck, I guess. Luckily, I was born optimistic and with a happy disposition. Having said that, it wasn't as if I was abused as a child: low level neglect is the worst acccusation I can throw at her. She loved me, I know: she just had an unusual way of showing it. Or not. I certainly don't want any pity, as millions of others have had it millions of times worse than me. The one thing writing this book has taught me – and hopefully, some of you – is that at least one of our parents will, almost inevitably, turn out to be flawed. Either a bit, or very deeply. And we should forgive them for it, learn to live with it, and not try to blame our own shortcomings on it.

It hasn't been easy writing this book, or justifying its existence. I still worry that maybe I should have left it buried. Unsaid. Undiscovered. But there is one very good reason indeed for writing it. By far and away the most important reason of all, in fact. It gives me and my family the chance to apologize. To the late Mr Stern, his family and anyone else who suffered any kind of discomfort, wrongdoing or distress as a result of my parents' actions, deliberate or otherwise: I am truly, truly sorry.

Acknowledgements

Special thanks to Adrian M. Melman, who pointed me in directions that I had never thought of going in, and who came up with invaluable insights, anecdotes and revelations. And my aunt, Ruthie, who gave it her blessing. If she hadn't, I wouldn't have done it. Thanks also to Lucian Randall, who read my first attempt and persuaded me it was worth carrying on with, when I didn't. Thank you also Humphrey Bowles. And everybody at Simon and Schuster, and in particular Kate Lyall Grant, the editor of this book, for backing it in the first place. Many thanks to the various members of the Stern family for being tolerant and helpful when they could quite easily have ignored me altogether, or worse. Katy Taylor-Richards: thank you for your indefatigable research, enthusiasm and tenacity. Michael and Judy Thomas, thank you for some Olympic standard proofreading. Thank *you*: for reading this book. And finally, thanks, of course, to my wife Emily for being lovely, loyal and supportive.